TIME
America
AN ILLUSTRATED HISTORY

LEWIS HINE—NY PUBLIC LIBRARY

America AN ILLUSTRATED HISTORY

EDITOR Kelly Knauer
INTRODUCTION Richard Stengel
DESIGNER Ellen Fanning
PICTURE EDITOR Patricia Cadley
WRITER/RESEARCH DIRECTOR Matthew McCann Fenton
COPY EDITOR Bruce Christopher Carr

TIME INC. HOME ENTERTAINMENT

PUBLISHER Richard Fraiman
GENERAL MANAGER Steven Sandonato
EXECUTIVE DIRECTOR, MARKETING SERVICES Carol Pittard
DIRECTOR, RETAIL & SPECIAL SALES Tom Mifsud
DIRECTOR, NEW PRODUCT DEVELOPMENT Peter Harper
ASSISTANT DIRECTOR, BRAND MARKETING Laura Adam
ASSISTANT GENERAL COUNSEL Dasha Smith Dwin
BOOK PRODUCTION MANAGER Jonathan Polsky
BRAND MANAGER Joy Butts
DESIGN AND PREPRESS MANAGER Anne-Michelle Gallero

SPECIAL THANKS

Bozena Bannett, Alexandra Bliss, Glenn Buonocore, Suzanne Janso, Robert Marasco, Brooke Reger, Shelley Rescober, Mary Sarro-Waite, Ilene Shreider, Adriana Tierno, Alex Voznesenskiy

Copyright 2007 Time Inc. Home Entertainment
Published by TIME Books
Time Inc. • 1271 Avenue of the Americas • New York, NY 10020

ISBN 10: 1-933821-24-8 • ISBN 13: 978-1-933821-24-5 • Library of Congress Number: 2007923882
TIME Books is a trademark of Time Inc.

We welcome your comments and suggestions about TIME Books. Please write to us at:
TIME Books
Attention: Book Editors
P.O. Box 11016
Des Moines, IA 50336-1016

If you would like to order any of our hardcover Collector's Edition books, please call us at 1-800-327-6388 (Monday through Friday, 7 a.m.–8 p.m., or Saturday, 7 a.m.–6 p.m., Central time).

PRINTED IN THE UNITED STATES OF AMERICA

Endpapers: © Tom Van Sant—GeoSphere Project—Corbis

Batter up! Photojournalist Lewis Hine documented the evils of child labor early in the 20th century; he also photographed children at play, as in this 1910 image of New York City tenement kids

Contents

iv

SMITHSONIAN INSTITUTION

The Old Ways These Blackfoot Indians in Montana were photographed in 1855. In the decades that followed, the Blackfoot people's nomadic way of life would be lost, as white settlement and aggressive hunting eliminated the great Western bison herds that were the basis of their culture

Memorable Images, Enduring Ideas

BY RICHARD STENGEL

PERHAPS THE MOST MEMORABLE ARGUMENT FOR CREATING A visual history of America was made by the notorious political master of late–19th century New York City, William (Boss) Tweed. As you will read on page 115, Tweed was outraged by the unflattering images of him created by editorial cartoonist Thomas Nast. "I don't care so much what the papers say," Tweed complained. "My constituents can't read, but damn it, they can see pictures!"

Telling America's story in pictures is a particularly American thing to do. For those of us who have grown up in the 20th century, American history seems like an epic newsreel set to a jazz and rock-'n'-roll soundtrack. From images of Washington crossing the Delaware to Lincoln in a top hat, from Babe Ruth clowning with an adoring kid to Martin Luther King Jr. marching for voting rights in Selma, Ala., we construct our own mental narrative of America in iconic images. For more than 80 years, TIME has helped tell that story with pictures that are both timely and timeless.

At the heart of that story is the American Dream, a dream far older than America itself. Centuries before Christopher Columbus' voyages, European cartographers placed the New World on their maps. The 18th century French-American author Hector St. John de Crèvecoeur linked geography to destiny when he called the American citizen the "New Man." America really was something new under the sun—not only a new land but also a new set of ideas.

In telling—and showing—the story of the New World, this book reflects an idea that TIME has always embraced: that of American exceptionalism. Unlike the nations of Europe, Americans were never bound by a common blood, background or religion. We were connected by an uncommon set of ideas, ideas articulated by Thomas Jefferson in the nation's birth certificate, the Declaration of Independence: that all men are created equal, that no man is above the law and that democracy derives its power from the consent of the governed. As Bono, the Irish rock star, likes to say, America is not so much a country as an idea.

That idea got its start 400 years ago in the settlement at Jamestown. The first permanent British colony in America not only established a foothold on this continent; it also helped create the DNA of what it means to be an American. It established a template for representative government, and it contained in embryo almost all the struggles and contradictions that have been at the heart of American history ever since. The European settlers, Native Americans and African slaves who came together in Jamestown's early years embodied the conflicts that would haunt America to the present day: the tension between liberty and equality, between the individual and the community, between isolationism and engagement, between man and nature, between North and South. At the same time, the Jamestown colony gave birth to one of the ideals that has helped us reckon with these challenges ever since: the abiding quest for liberty and freedom.

The book also mirrors the ways in which American history at every stage was transformed by technology, from the long rifle of the colonists to the cannons of the Civil War to the railroad that opened up commerce and the American West. Walt Whitman said democracy would create its own art forms, and it did, in a series of innovative formats: photography, radio, film, television and now the World Wide Web. The earliest images of America were painted landscapes that displayed to the Old World what the New World looked like. But it was that most democratic of arts, photography, that would bring America alive to the rest of the world. From the grim images of the battlefield at Antietam, which first showed the horror of modern warfare, to the bleak scenes of the Depression to the flag being raised on Iowa Jima, photography became America's signature art form, one that was accessible to all.

We tend to think of history as being written in stone. But history, like science, is not static but dynamic. It is changed not only by new discoveries but also by the perspectives of the present. This book is less a history than a brisk newsreel of the great sweep of the American narrative. Whitman celebrated himself as a microcosm of America, and these pages celebrate the highs and the lows of the American experience. "I contain multitudes," Whitman boasted, and so does this book: multitudes of ideas, of people and places, of disasters and dreams, all of which form a teeming mosaic of American life and history. After all, as Whitman wrote, "the United States is essentially the greatest poem." We just combined that poetry with pictures. ∎

— *Richard Stengel is the Managing Editor of* TIME *magazine.*

Faded Glory: This hand-painted campaign banner promoted Democratic-Republican Party candidate Thomas Jefferson for the presidency over his rival from the Federalist Party, John Adams. The message reads, JEFFERSON FOR PRESIDENT, ADAMS NO MORE. Jefferson and Adams collaborated with Benjamin Franklin and two others to write the Declaration of Independence in 1776, but the two later became political rivals. Adams was elected the nation's second President, and Jefferson served two terms as its third. In later life, the two men forged a lasting friendship through correspondence; both died on the 50th anniversary of the signing of the Declaration, on July 4, 1826.

AMERICAE SIVE NOVI ORBIS, NOVA DESCRIPTIO.

A New World

THE AMERICAN DREAM IS OLDER THAN AMERICA. CENTURIES before Christopher Columbus' historic 1492 voyage put the New World on European maps, the Old World was buzzing with stories of lands beyond the western horizon. These fables depicted wilderness realms, rich with resources—Edenic gardens freed from Europe's burden of history. Even before Spanish conquistadors, French trappers, Dutch navigators and English colonists began charting the terrain of the New World in the 16th century, it was viewed as a land of opportunity, where both a single man and all of mankind might start life over again.

Many of the first English colonists came to America in search of a life blessed with riches; others sought a life rich in blessings. But all came in search of a better life. Scholars call this sense that America has been set aside for a special, beneficial destiny in the world "American exceptionalism." It has helped define the United States from before there were states and before they were united.

The map at left was made in 1570 by Abraham Ortelius; it would be 300 more years before the landscape of the American West was fully explored. To European eyes, this *Orbis Nova* was a blank slate waiting to be filled in by white settlement. That vision ignored the millions of natives already residing in the Americas; European settlers would turn a similarly blind eye to the African slaves they began using as laborers as early as 1619. Today we regard the history of America as not only a story of politics but also a story of cultures and races. It is the story of three distinct peoples— Native Americans, European Americans and African Americans— and of their long struggle to build an exceptional nation, a nation a later American would describe as "conceived in liberty and dedicated to the proposition that all men are created equal."

"I always consider the settlement of America with reverence and wonder, as the opening of a grand scene and design in providence, for the illumination of the ignorant and the emancipation of the slavish part of mankind all over the earth." —JOHN ADAMS, 1765

3

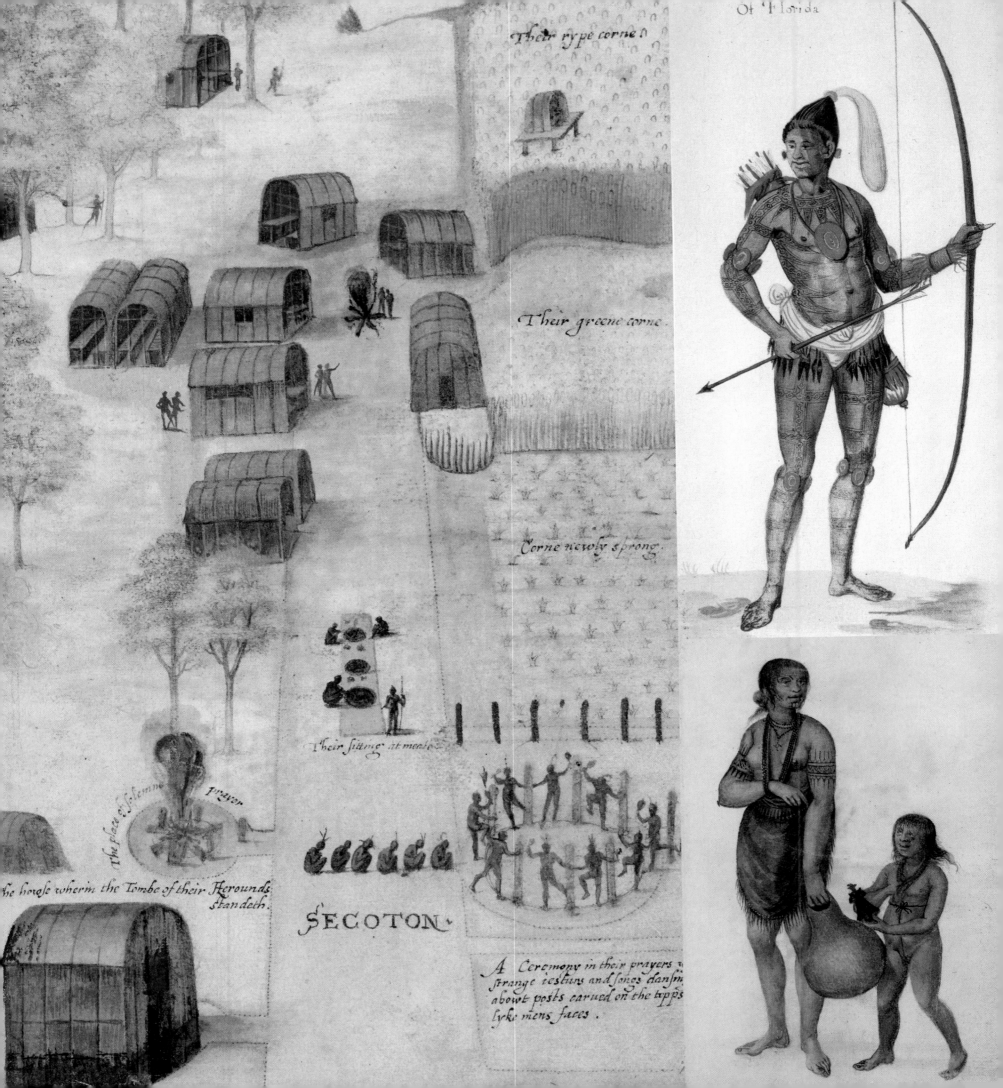

Their rype corne

Their greene corne.

Corne newly sprong.

Their sitting at meate.

The place of solemne prayer.

he house wherin the Tombe of their Herounds standeth.

SECOTON.

A Ceremony in their prayers w
strange iestures and songs dansin
abowt posts carued on the topps
lyke mens faces.

Of Florida

The flyer

Close Encounters, First Impressions • 1585

The white Europeans who first came to America were pursuing the myth of an unimaginably rich New World that was, as if by divine intervention or magic, falling into the hands of those who were destined to settle and civilize it. While many myths contain a grain of truth, this one was amost entirely false. The New World had been settled and civilized for at least 25,000 years before Columbus first crossed the Atlantic; the first ancestors of Native Americans arrived, probably via the Bering Strait, from Asia. In the centuries that followed, they journeyed across the western hemisphere, branching off into hundreds of separate nations, empires and tribes.

But one man's civilization can be another man's savagery. Following in the path of Spanish conquistadors who explored the southern reaches of today's U.S. early in the 16th century, a group of British adventurers landed near today's Roanoke, Va., in hopes of founding a moneymaking colony in 1585. The clash of cultures that followed is documented in these paintings of native peoples by colonist John White, which depict Native Americans fishing, hunting and feasting. To White and his colleagues, the Indians were savages, and whites so viewed them for centuries; Thomas Jefferson wrote of "merciless Indian savages" in the Declaration of Independence.

The Roanoke colony failed, but the impact of the first encounters between Europeans and Native Americans was profound. More than a million Indians died in the first 100 years of European settlement in the New World after they were exposed to ailments not present in the Americas. Their grim fate helped convince the new residents of the validity of the dark premise of their arrival: that all the land's native peoples were simply going to vanish, as the inexorable logic of European expansion barreled on.

TOP: UNIVERSITY OF VIRGINIA; LEFT, FROM LEFT: APVA PRESERVATION VIRGINIA (3)

Emblems of Colonial Life

Misled by early settlers' maps, scholars long believed the original fort at Jamestown was now underwater, but in 1993 archaeologist William Kelso began unearthing artifacts from the settlement's earliest days on dry land. From left are an English Border Ware drinking jug, an English sixpence and a German-made brass thimble.

American Slavery Takes Root in Jamestown

If slavery was America's original sin, Jamestown was where the sin originated. In 1619 about 20 Africans from what is now Angola were sold to settlers of the fledgling colony, who were still trying to develop an economy. Initially, field labor in Virginia was provided by white indentured servants; like slaves, they were bought and sold, but were less expensive, since they were set free in 7 years. By the 1660s, however, increased supplies made it cheaper to buy African slaves than white indentures, and the former were also considered less rebellious. By 1769, the date of the poster at right, slavery was essential to Southern life.

So emerged one of the great contradictions of American history. Southerners, whose region boasted the most vibrant democracy and the largest electorate, were committed to large-scale slavery and insisted there was no inconsistency between liberty for most and slavery for some. For black Americans the results were tragic and lasting. Jamestown's creation instilled in the broader culture the belief that African Americans, even though they were among the land's earliest arrivals, were to be forever excluded from all basic rights of citizenship.

In the Jamestown Colony, Settlers Plant the Seeds of American History

In 2007 Americans celebrated the 400th anniversary of the founding of Jamestown, the first lasting British settlement in the U.S. Its settlers were lured across the Atlantic by the prospect of riches: imagine that today's Congress gave Wal-Mart and General Electric permission to colonize Mars, and you will have some idea of the capitalist motives that led to the new colony's founding. At a time when the Spanish, French and Portuguese were getting rich on America's lumber, silver and furs, respectively, the London Co., a group of merchants with a royal patent, sponsored 104 English settlers—gentlemen, soldiers, privateers, artisans, laborers and boys (but no women)—as late entrants in the burgeoning New World sweepstakes.

The colonists' first few years were marked by disease, starvation and Indian attacks, but in short order, Jamestown became the first New World colony to find a cash cow and an economic system for exploiting it. The nearby Powhatan Indians smoked a crude indigenous species of tobacco. But in 1612, colonist John Rolfe imported seeds of *Nicotiana tabacum,* the Spanish-American weed that was already a craze in England. By 1620 the colony had shipped almost 50,000 lbs. of tobacco home. Jamestown's success also bred myths, such as the familiar, if often overly embellished, story of the Indian girl Pocahontas saving the life of the colony's swaggering Captain John Smith, as depicted in the 1874 lithograph at left.

The colony's most far-reaching innovation, however, was representative government. In 1618 the Virginia Co. created a general assembly to advise the Governor; from this seed would grow the House of Burgesses, the elective house of Virginia's colonial legislature. One year later a new workforce, African slaves, began tending the tobacco crops. In their rough-and-ready way, the Jamestown settlers had planted the seeds of a dynamic system, democratic capitalism, along with an institution that would pervert it, chattel slavery, and a force that would supply the cure, the goal of liberty.

In the North, Settlers Seek a Safe Harbor for Religious Dissent

The New World lured not only Britons in pursuit of riches but also those seeking to put a wide ocean between themselves and the established Anglican Church. The Virginia colonists lured some Dissenters (radical Protestants, who had already fled to Holland) to Jamestown and opened negotiations with others. One boatload of these Pilgrims, blown north, landed in today's Plymouth, Mass., in 1620. These Northern colonists would make religious devotion a priority for long years to come, while Virginians continued to develop their plantation economy. This division, increasingly widened by the Southern embrace of slavery, helped shape the North-South dichotomy that would forge America's future.

Five years after the landing at Plymouth, Boston was founded on a fine natural harbor; by 1722, when William Burgis made the first known sketch of it, above, Boston was the largest city in the New World.

A Global War of Empires Shapes America's Destiny

Residents of Britain's North American colonies called the 18th century showdown that decided America's future the French and Indian War, but Europeans referred to it by the name of the larger imperial chess game of which it was but a small part: the Seven Years War. The conflict was started in 1754 by a 21-year-old Virginia militia officer named George Washington, who was assigned to evict French settlers deemed to be trespassing on land in the Ohio River Valley claimed by Britain. The French refused to leave, shots were fired, and a full-scale struggle for control of the New World ensued; it soon spread to become a global conflict, engulfing Europe, Africa, India and the Philippines.

In the war's North American theater, the British suffered a rough start against the French but soon found their footing. By 1758, they were laying siege to Quebec, below, where Britain's General James Wolfe inflicted a crushing defeat on the French commander, the Marquis de Montcalm. Both leaders were mortally wounded in the battle; at right, Montcalm dies. Native Americans fought on both sides of the conflict: while the French commanded the allegiance of a larger number of tribes, the powerful Iroquois Confederacy proved valuable allies for the British.

At the war's end, America's future was sealed: the French lost Canada and its string of forts stretching along the Mississippi River down to New Orleans. France's ally, Spain, surrendered Florida but kept Mexico and vast lands west of the Mississippi River (which it later ceded back to France). And the British gained control of all North America east of the Mississippi River. And that is why, 240 years later, this book is written in English rather than French.

8

The BLOODY MASSACRE perpetrated in King—Street BOSTON on March 5th 1770 by a party of the 29th REGt

Colonies in Crisis and Bloodshed in Boston

To pay the debts from the long war with France, London imposed heavy taxes on her American colonies. But colonists who were prospering in a society that rewarded personal initiative felt increasingly cramped by the strictures of a faraway Parliament where their voices were unheard. Britain's protection, essential in the time of war, now seemed oppressive. Colonial resentment of taxes led to widespread smuggling, coupled with threats against royal tax collectors. In 1768 Britain's governor in Massachusetts was forced to call in troops to quell unruly Boston, the largest city in the colonies.

In a city of 16,000, the appearance of more than 4,000 British soldiers rankled—especially when they began competing with locals for part-time work. Tensions boiled over on March 5, 1770, when a rioting crowd threatened two British sentries—and in the melee that followed, five Americans were shot dead. The incident, branded the Boston Massacre, became a rallying point for colonial patriots. The engraving at left by Boston silversmith Paul Revere (inspired largely by another work) served as propaganda, falsifying several details in the Americans' favor. But Revere's engraving had its intended effect: even colonists who were inclined to sympathize with Britain were outraged by the killings.

9

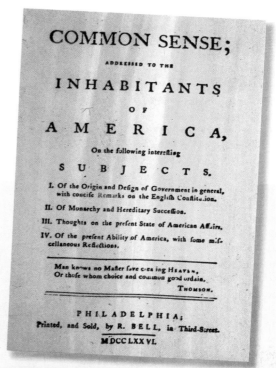

Come Together, Right Now

In 1754, Benjamin Franklin published one of America's first political cartoons in the *Pennsylvania Gazette*. Intended as a commentary on "the present disunited state of the British Colonies," Franklin's drawing had nothing to do with American independence; it was intended to exhort colonists to unite against France during the French and Indian War. (Popular superstition held that a snake cut in two would come back to life if the pieces were joined before dusk.)

Franklin republished the cartoon in 1765. But in the 11 years since it was created, the image now took on an entirely different meaning: as Americans were loudly protesting new British taxes decreed under the hated Stamp Act, the cartoon called upon colonists to unite against England. In the next decade, the image would make a third appearance—this time on the flags of patriot armies, with the slogan Don't Tread On Me.

A Call for Freedom Becomes a Call to Arms

Early in 1776, as colonial resentment of England was turning into outright rebellion, Franklin urged the gifted British writer Thomas Paine to publish *Common Sense*, a brief pamphlet that electrified the colonies by casting the struggle for colonial independence as a milestone in world history. Paine's potent broadside led directly to the Declaration of Independence.

"Justice is the end of government. It is the end of civil society. It ever has been and ever will be pursued until it be obtained, or until liberty be lost in the pursuit." —JAMES MADISON, FEDERALIST NO. 51, 1788

1776-1800

Birth of a Nation

WHEN THE MEN OF BRITAIN'S 13 COLONIES IN AMERICA MARCHED OFF TO FIGHT FOR THEIR FREEDOM, as imagined in this sentimentalized late–19th century illustration, they were joining a movement whose shattering impact on history still resounds. For theirs was not merely a political revolution: it was also a revolution in consciousness, as people who had flourished under relative freedom began to envision a society based on inherent human rights, in which the government existed to serve the individual rather than vice versa. The patriots' call to arms, the U.S. Declaration of Independence, might have been only a simple brief of Britain's "abuses and usurpations"; instead it became a sweeping call for people everywhere to demand their rights as human beings and create radical new kinds of government that guaranteed personal liberties, cultivated opportunity and dispensed justice to all citizens as equals.

Freedom: A Work in Progress • 1776

It's tempting to think of the 13 colonies' historic Declaration of Independence from Britain as having been handed down like biblical tablets, polished and perfect. The truth is more messy, as Thomas Jefferson's handwritten draft at left, heavily revised and scrawled over, illustrates. Meeting in Philadelphia in 1776, the Continental Congress, below, asked Jefferson (then only 33), John Adams, Benjamin Franklin and two others to draw up the argument for ending colonial ties to Britain. Their labors are reflected at left: Franklin crossed out part of chief author Jefferson's statement "We hold these truths to be sacred and undeniable" in favor of "We hold these truths to be self-evident," changing their origin from a divine gift to a rational conclusion.

The Declaration's primary tenet, that "all men are created equal," would ring down through history, defying monarchies and totalitarian societies by elevating the individual's rights over those of the state and inspiring revolutionaries, suffragists and abolitionists around the globe. As radical now as then, those five words still challenge Americans to live up to their promise of equal justice and opportunity for all.

12

THE FOUNDING FATHERS: AMERICA'S GREATEST GENERATION

An unlikely band of rebels—including Southern plantation owners, Northern lawyers and an outcast British polemicist—came together in the 1770s, united by a common cause: anger over imperial Britain's cavalier treatment of its 13 thriving colonies in America

13

Rebels with a Cause

America's Founding Fathers compose a rich, fascinating cross-section of colonial life. Clock-wise from top left, George Washington was a Virginia planter who had the most military experience of the rebel colonials and was the natural choice to lead the fledgling patriot armies. Samuel Adams of Massachusetts, an outspoken activist and rabble rouser, was a leader of the Boston Tea Party in 1773.

Thomas Paine, a Briton, inspired the rebels with his incisive 1776 polemic *Common Sense,* whose principles helped shape the Declaration of Independence. Virginia's Thomas Jefferson wrote the stirring Declaration in only three weeks, aided by John Adams of Massachusetts, a brilliant, cantankerous lawyer who would become the nation's second President.

A Daring Attack Restores American Hopes • 1776

The Declaration of Independence launched America into a full-fledged war of revolution that seemed a lopsided match from the outset, as 13 wildly diverse colonies, with no standing army or navy, faced the full power of the world's most potent imperial war machine. And sure enough: after 20,000 British troops and mercenaries landed on Long Island on Aug. 26, 1776, they routed General George Washington's green soldiers in a hat trick of victories at Long Island, Manhattan and White Plains. The outnumbered patriots fled through New Jersey and across the Delaware River into Pennsylvania, their numbers depleted to 6,000, half their original strength.

The British came very close at this time to strangling the incipient revolution before it fully coalesced. With some one-third of all the British colonists remaining loyal to the King; with the important port of New York City in Britain's hands; and with Washington's small, underfunded army on the run, the British had every right to believe that they would soon bring the upstart American colonists to heel.

In December the British and the German mercenaries in their employ, the Hessians, entered winter quarters along the Delaware near Trenton, N.J., awaiting spring and a final campaign to finish off the rebellion: Britain's Lord Cornwallis bragged that he would bag George Washington the way a hunter snags a fox. At this critical juncture, Washington took the offensive. Gathering a small force, he slipped across the ice-choked river into New Jersey late on Christmas night and launched a surprise attack early on Dec. 26 that caught the Hessians, glutted with holiday wassail, napping. The gambit succeeded, giving the soldiers—and all U.S. patriots—a much needed sense that Washington's army was a real fighting force, capable, imaginative and stealthy. There would be no quick finish to the American rebellion.

One Event, Many Visions

Washington's secret nighttime crossing of the Delaware River became a favorite subject for American painters; on these pages, we see two very different realizations of the scene. The version at left was published by the influential lithography house of Currier & Ives in 1876, 100 years after the event took place. The version above is a copy of an 1851 work by the German-American painter Emanuel Leutze. In both cases, the artists were working entirely from their imagination, unhindered by close familiarity with the events they depicted.

Leutze's rendering of the scene, above, is one of the most familiar images of American patriotic iconography. It is filled with historical errors, for the artist's goal was not to show how the event really looked but to show how it *should* have looked. So Washington's boat carries the Stars and Stripes flag—even though that flag had not yet been created in 1776. The Currier & Ives image, if equally imagined, at least captures more of the feel of a ragtag band of brothers launching an all-or-nothing wintertime attack against great odds.

The differences between the pictures remind us that many of our mental images of the first 60 years of U.S. history are based on visions imagined by their creators long after the events they depict, before photography brought a new level of realism to history. Indeed, many of the familiar stories of the Revolutionary era—the brave female warrior Molly Pitcher, the flagmaker Betsy Ross, Washington's refusal to lie to his father—were constructs of patriotic 19th century Americans, intent on creating memorable tales of the nation's founding that would appeal to children. In stripping away the gaudy embellishments of such stories, modern scholars and historians are finding no lack of authentic heroism and valor in the nation's early years: Washington's crossing doesn't need to fly under a false flag to merit our admiration.

A Seesaw Contest • 1777

Striking quickly to take advantage of his brilliant stratagem in routing the Hessians on Dec. 26, 1776, George Washington next attacked the main body of British troops garrisoned at nearby Princeton, N.J., on Jan. 3, 1777. The second surprise victory sent British troops reeling backward, eventually forcing them to abandon most of New Jersey. It also bolstered patriot hopes: Washington's army swelled with some 6,000 volunteers.

On Sept. 11, 1777, Washington engaged the British in a more formal battle near Brandywine, Pa., left. Fighting on their terms, the Britons whipped the colonial troops and captured a prize, Philadelphia.

Winter at Valley Forge • 1777-78

Washington's army was defeated at Brandywine, but good news for patriots came from a different front in the next six weeks: at Saratoga in upstate New York, colonial soldiers defeated a British army invading the colonies from Canada; more than 6,000 Redcoats surrendered.

On the southern front, the British wintered in Philadelphia in 1777-78, while Washington's troops camped only 20 miles north of them, in Valley Forge, Pa., left. Here, aided by two able European professionals, France's Marquis de Lafayette and Prussia's Friedrich Von Steuben, Washington used his time well, turning his force of amateur recruits into professional soldiers.

Turning Point at Cowpens • 1781

With the tide of war running against the British in the Northern colonies, London shifted its strategic focus to securing its hold over the South. The Britons initially met with success, capturing two colonial crown jewels, Savannah, Ga., in December 1778 and Charleston, S.C., the following May. But the Redcoat advance was turned back by a decisive colonial victory at Cowpens, S.C., left, in January 1781.

The defeat pushed Britain's General Charles Cornwallis to retreat toward Virginia, where he hoped that the Royal Navy could evacuate his army to British-held New York City through the port of Yorktown.

16

The Rebels Prevail: A Beaten Empire Signs the Treaty of Paris • 1781-83

In the autumn of 1781 General Cornwallis' army had its back to the sea at Yorktown, Va., when his exit was blocked by the surprise arrival of a French fleet: as Britain's enemy, the French supported the colonial cause. A month-long siege of Yorktown by Washington and France's General Jean-Baptiste Rochambeau persuaded Cornwallis to concede not only the city but also his campaign; above, he surrenders on Oct. 19.

Against all odds, and after five years of battles, the colonials had won the war, although its official conclusion did not come until 1783, when American diplomats, including John Adams, John Jay and Benjamin Franklin, signed the Treaty of Paris, right. The rebels' hardest work lay ahead: governing a new nation.

18

Constructing a Federal City • 1799

A new nation called for a new capital city, but the states squabbled over which of them would receive the honor—and economic boost—of hosting the young government. A 1790 compromise brokered by Virginians Thomas Jefferson and James Madison and New Yorker Alexander Hamilton resolved the issue and also addressed the states' divisions over slavery and war debts from the Revolution. The new capital would be placed on land carved from two Southern states, Maryland and Virginia, and named the District of Columbia. In return the Federal Government, rather than the individual states, would pay the lingering debts from the Revolutionary War, as the North preferred. One key point was clearly understood but not written down: the North would not propose outlawing slavery in the South.

The capital was named for the hero of the war, and a grand, sweeping plan for it, right, was laid out by French-born architect Pierre L'Enfant; construction began in 1791. The 1799 sketch above shows the unfinished "President's Palace"; President John Adams moved into the executive mansion in 1801. It would be captured and burned 13 years later by the British in the War of 1812.

Constructing a Constitution • 1787-89

In America's first years of freedom, the newly forged union of states was poorly prepared to govern itself. The Articles of Confederation and Perpetual Union adopted in 1781 called for a very weak Federal Government that could not levy taxes, pass laws or raise an army. As problems grew, the Founding Fathers gathered in 1787 in Philadelphia to hammer out a new Constitution. The key principles of the version they approved continue to define the U.S. government: the division into Executive, Judicial and Legislative branches; a two-branch legislature; and the Electoral College system of choosing a President.

But one problem persisted: the new document was missing a key element, a Bill of Rights to guarantee individual freedoms. When the proposed Constitution's supporters—including the authors of the series of 85 *Federalist* papers, below, James Madison (inset), John Jay and Alexander Hamilton—agreed to include a Bill of Rights as the first 10 Amendments to the Constitution, the new system of government was ratified in 1789. To no one's surprise, George Washington was elected the first President that year.

19

WHAT ONE FATHER FOUNDED

If the term Renaissance Man hadn't already been coined, it might have been invented to describe Benjamin Franklin. The energetic Philadelphian founded America's first lending library, first fire department and first hospital. He didn't create, but did greatly improve, the colonies' rudimentary postal system. Franklin also played a major role in establishing two separate institutions of higher learning: the University of Pennsylvania and Franklin and Marshall College. In his "spare time," he wrote his autobiography; even though unfinished, it is a classic of the genre.

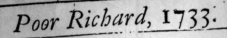

Poor Richard, 1733.
AN
Almanack
For the Year of Chrift
1733,
Being the Firft after LEAP YEAR:

And makes fince the Creation	Years
By the Account of the Eaftern *Greeks*	7241
By the Latin Church, when ☉ ent. ♈	6932
By the Computation of *W.W.*	5742
By the *Roman* Chronology	5682
By the *Jewifh* Rabbies	5494

Wherein is contained
The Lunations, Eclipfes, Judgment of the Weather, Spring Tides, Planets Motions & mutual Afpects, Sun and Moon's Rifing and Setting, Length of Days, Time of High Water, Fairs, Courts, and obfervable Days.
Fitted to the Latitude of Forty Degrees, and a Meridian of Five Hours Weft from *London*, but may without fenfible Error, ferve all the adjacent Places, even from *Newfoundland* to *South-Carolina*.
By RICHARD SAUNDERS, Philom.

PHILADELPHIA:
Printed and fold by *B. FRANKLIN*, at the New Printing-Office near the Market.

Richard's Almanack

...ning in 1733, Franklin published 25 ...al editions of his almanac. A runaway best ... of the era, it often sold more than 10,000 ...s a year. Valued for its calendars, weather ...sts and astronomical tables, it was also ... for its wit and homespun wisdom, much ...rrowed from other sources. The annual ...e's championing of thrift and moderation ...ted for its upwardly mobile readership, ... its pleasure-loving publisher generally ...ed to ignore his own advice.

Benjamin Franklin, American Archetype

For most of his life, Benjamin Franklin personified everything that young America could be but hadn't yet become. The single most famous person in the colonies, and the only one most Europeans knew by name before the revolution, Franklin was an intellectually curious inventor and scientist, a successful printer and publisher, a gifted politician (whose penchant for compromise also made him a natural diplomat) and a prodigious founder of institutions. His embodiment of America's potential not only helped spark the creation of the new nation but also inspired the fledgling Republic to live up to its own ideals.

Born in Boston in 1706, Franklin moved to Philadelphia to apprentice with his older brother, a printer; he founded his own newspaper, the *Pennsylvania Gazette*, at age 17. It was soon the most successful newspaper in colonial America. Always active in politics, he was appointed by the colony of Pennsylvania to represent its interests in England in 1757. Several other colonies soon hired Franklin in the same capacity, and he quickly became an unofficial ambassador for all of them. Living in London for 18 years, he became famous among Europeans for his charm, brilliance and scientific achievements, and he argued ably against Britain's repressive measures against the colonies, such as the Stamp Act.

Franklin returned to America in 1775 and became a forceful advocate for colonial freedom, collaborating with Thomas Jefferson to write the Declaration of Independence. The following year, he went to Europe once again, this time representing the American cause in Paris, where he was instrumental in securing French funds and troops to aid the revolution. In 1784 he came back to the young nation he had done so much to create and helped broker the compromises that led to the ratification of the U.S. Constitution. His last public act before his death in 1790 was to sign a statement arguing for the abolition of slavery.

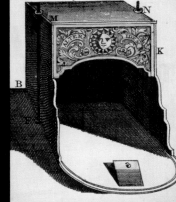

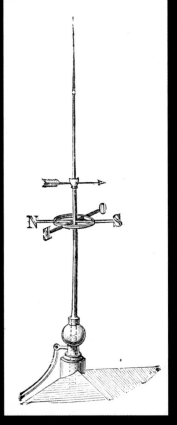

Bifocals

Tired of switching from one pair of spectacles to another, depending on whether he needed to see up close or at a distance, amateur inventor Franklin devised the first process for grinding two different types of lenses into a single piece of glass in the early 1760s.

Franklin Stove

Since fireplaces throw heat in only one direction, Franklin designed a cast-iron stove to stand in the middle of a room and radiate warmth in all directions—while creating more heat from less wood than other stoves.

Lightning Rod

A leading scientist of electricity, Franklin realized that metal could draw "electrical fire" from the clouds. His invention thwarted a major cause of injury and damage in an era of wooden buildings.

A Battle at Fallen Timbers Pushes Indians West • 1794

Native Americans who found themselves displaced from their homes and hunting grounds by the ongoing influx of white settlement in the colonies often fought alongside the British in the Revolutionary War. The colonials' stunning victory further increased the pressure on the Indians, who fought back in the Northwest Indian War.

After Indian victories in 1791 and '92, President George Washington sent General "Mad Anthony" Wayne and some 5,000 troops to fight an Indian coalition led by, among others, the revered Mohawk chief Joseph Brant, inset. At the critical Battle of Fallen Timbers, near present-day Toledo, Ohio, U.S. troops and cavalry routed the Indians on Aug. 20, 1794, securing the Ohio Territory for the U.S. and helping tamp down violence along the frontier for two decades.

Daniel Boone Leads the Way West

The colonists who united in revolution against Britain perched along the Eastern shore of an immense landmass about which they knew very little. To the west were great forests and the mighty river that divided the continent, the Mississippi. Beyond that were vast, blank spaces on colonial maps; far to the southwest was Spain's colony of Mexico. The Northwest Territory—the area that later would be carved up into today's Midwestern states—was roamed in the Republic's early days only by Native Americans and a few hearty white trappers and settlers, as was the vast mountain wilderness that would later become the states of Kentucky and Tennessee.

The movement of whites into these lands was led by frontiersman Daniel Boone (1734-1820), who cleared a walking route through the Cumberland Gap in the Appalachian Mountains from Virginia into Tennessee and Kentucky along an old Indian trail in 1775; he widened it for wagons in 1795. At left is his first journey, as imagined by mid–19th century artist George Caleb Bingham, whose Boone seems attired more for the parlor than the frontier.

Jefferson's Heritage: Ideals and Realities

In 1776, even as Thomas Jefferson was writing in the Declaration of Independence that "all men are created equal," the young Virginia planter owned some 100 slaves. Jefferson was aware of the dichotomy between his idealistic words and the brutalities of slavery; he wrote of human bondage in his 1781 book *Notes on the State of Virginia:* "I tremble for my country when I reflect that God is just." One of his slaves was the man shown in this 1847 daguerreotype, Isaac Jefferson, who was born around 1775. Set free four years before Jefferson died in 1826, Isaac moved to Petersburg, Va., where he worked as a blacksmith; proud of his status as a free laborer, he posed for his portrait in his work apron, with his tools.

The notion that Thomas Jefferson could have fathered children by his slaves might have been scoffed at as recently as the 1980s, but DNA testing on modern-day Americans has now shown that that is the case. In 2003, some of those descendants were welcomed at the Jefferson family reunion at the celebrated Virginia mansion he designed, Monticello.

"We can no longer say there is nothing new under the sun. For this whole chapter in the history of man is new. The great extent of our republic is new. Its sparse habitation is new."

—THOMAS JEFFERSON, PRIVATE LETTER, 1801

1800-40

The Young Republic

WHEN REVOLUTIONARY WAR LEGEND GEORGE WASHINGTON HANDED OVER THE PRESIDENCY OF THE U.S. to John Adams in 1797, Europeans were astonished: the peaceful transition of power proved that the upstart Americans really had invented a new form of democratic government. Then again, in those days almost every aspect of life in the young North American republic was new: its laws; its political parties; its unprecedented personal freedoms, as set out in the Bill of Rights; its sizable frontier, beckoning the adventurous West. Then, in 1803, President Thomas Jefferson purchased the Louisiana Territory from France, with one bold stroke doubling the size of the nation.

In the years that followed, Americans would be tested by war with the British, by troubles between white settlers and the Native Americans they were increasingly displacing and by sectional disputes over the practice of slavery. But the Clark Fork River shown here, named for explorer William Clark, and the entire Louisiana Purchase of which it was a part, promised Americans that their nation would have a vast new frontier to provide growing room, opportunity and resources for decades to come. A nation founded on expansive hopes and ideals now boasted the size to match them.

Lewis and Clark Explore a Vast New Frontier • 1804-06

When the Louisiana Purchase agreement between the U.S. and France was formally ratified in October 1803, the extent of America's territory was doubled overnight, increasing the nation's size by more than 820,000 sq. mi.—at a bargain-basement price of around 4¢ an acre. Eventually, all or part of 13 new U.S. states would be carved out of this sweeping wilderness.

Even before U.S. diplomats in Paris finished negotiating the transaction, the ever curious President Thomas Jefferson gave a trusted aide, Meriwether Lewis, the mission of exploring the new lands, hoping in part to find a waterway linking America's greatest river and the Pacific Ocean. Lewis enlisted his close friend and military comrade, William Clark, to lead the expedition with him. Departing from St. Louis in May 1804, the company of more than 20 men wintered in what is now North Dakota, where they luckily encountered Sacajawea, a Shoshone Indian woman who became their guide. The company crossed the Rocky Mountains in August 1805 and reached the Pacific three months later. On their return to St. Louis in September 1806, the explorers were greeted as national heroes. On this page is a fanciful illustration of their journey by a popular later–19th century painter, Thomas Mickell Burnham. If imagined by the artist, it succeeds in capturing the sense of a wilderness at dawn in a period of morning in America.

Tools of the Explorers' Trade

As explorers commissioned by polymath President Thomas Jefferson, Lewis and Clark kept scrupulously complete journals—13 volumes of them—which chronicle their adventures in detail: the Indians they met, the streams they forded, the weather they endured, the animals they shot and the flowers they admired. At right is a medal commissioned by Jefferson for his representatives to give to the Indians, as a sign of U.S. good faith. At left, a compass used by the company.

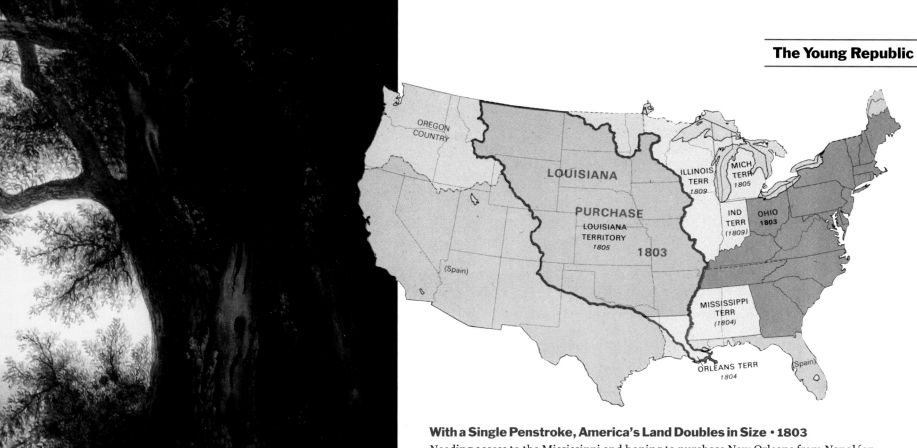

With a Single Penstroke, America's Land Doubles in Size • 1803

Needing access to the Mississippi and hoping to purchase New Orleans from Napoléon Bonaparte, President Jefferson sent U.S. diplomats to Paris early in 1803, authorizing them to spend up to $10 million. Instead, they wrote a check for $15 million and came back with the deed for vast lands west of the Mississippi, in green above. The western border of the territory was left hazy, so as not to antagonize Spain, whose Mexican colonies the area bordered—and also because neither European nor American whites were familiar with the area's geography.

27

Sacajawea, the Pathfinder

The Lewis and Clark expedition succeeded thanks to a welcome instance of cooperation between whites and Native Americans: Sacajawea, a Shoshone woman of around 16, blazed the trail from today's North Dakota to the Pacific Northwest, more than once saving her companions from disaster. When the guide fell ill once, Lewis confided to his diary: "if this woman dies, our mission may fail." Along the way, the wife of a French interpreter gave birth to a son, whom she carried for the rest of the long journey.

28

The U.S. and Britain March to War Again • 1812-15

After the U.S. declared war on Britain in 1812, angered by British impressment of U.S. sailors and border disputes with Canada, a confused, sprawling conflict ensued. President James Madison hoped Britain's ongoing war with France would divert the English and that parts of Canada might be annexed by the U.S., but he guessed wrong: Canada remained in British hands, while the enemy briefly occupied and burned Washington, above, in 1814. But a later British naval invasion of Baltimore was repelled, and General Andrew Jackson handily defeated a British army in 1815's Battle of New Orleans, left, which took place several weeks after peace was reached, thanks to the era's slow-moving news. In reality the U.S. gained little from the war, but Jackson's late victory convinced Americans they had again whipped the empire.

Dawn's Early Light • 1814

"Does not such a country ... deserve a song?" lawyer Francis Scott Key would recall thinking during the night he spent in custody aboard a British warship, watching the bombardment of Baltimore's Fort McHenry, below. The battle inspired his patriotic poem that begins, "O say can you see, by the dawn's early light?"

Happily, the sight of the U.S. flag still waving over the fort's ramparts as the sun rose on Sept. 14, 1814, indeed signaled that the stronghold hadn't fallen. Key's words were set to the melody of a British drinking song and given a new title: *The Star-Spangled Banner;* the song was officially declared the national anthem in 1931. The 15-star flag Key hailed so proudly, right, is preserved at the Smithsonian Institution.

29

Battle at Tippecanoe • 1811

At a clearing where the Tippecanoe Creek empties into the Wabash River, deep within the Indiana Territory, Native American leader Tecumseh, right—a charismatic Shawnee warrior chief and the twin brother of a shaman regarded as a prophet—gathered an army in the summer of 1811, determined to defend Indian land against the rising tide of white settlers. Tecumseh believed his dream of forging a confederation of all the Indian tribes threatened by the whites' westward expansion would be within reach if he could score a single dramatic victory. His forces attacked those commanded by U.S. General William Henry Harrison on Nov. 7, 1811, above.

Both sides suffered heavy losses in the fray, but the U.S. Army didn't need to score a knockout blow to survive, and Tecumseh did. His dreams of Indian unity died that day, and Tecumseh himself died two years later, fighting in Canada on the side of the British during the War of 1812. Harrison was elected President in 1840, and the Indians of the Midwestern forests continued on their long journey toward the setting sun.

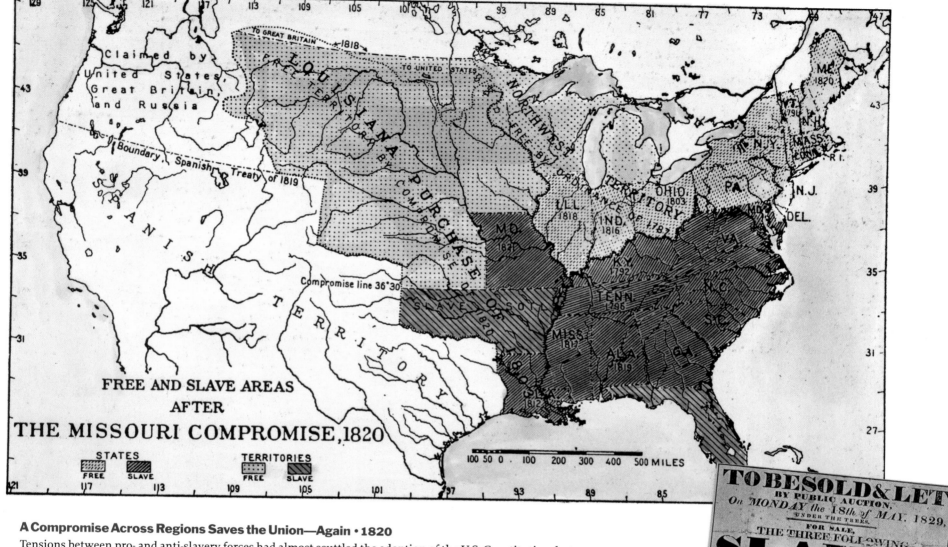

FREE AND SLAVE AREAS
AFTER
THE MISSOURI COMPROMISE, 1820

STATES   TERRITORIES
FREE   SLAVE   FREE   SLAVE

100 50 0 · 100   200   300   400   500 MILES

A Compromise Across Regions Saves the Union—Again • 1820

Tensions between pro- and anti-slavery forces had almost scuttled the adoption of the U.S. Constitution, but a 1790 compromise over the placement of the nation's capital city held the North and South together. Yet slavery was too hot an issue to be tamped down by a single political pact; it sparked controversy for the next three decades. Regional rivalries reached a boiling point in 1819, when the Missouri Territory sought to join the Union as a slaveholding state, at a time when the 22 existing states were evenly divided between slave and free factions, above.

After months of bitter debate, Kentucky Senator Henry Clay brokered a compromise in which Missouri was admitted to the Union as a slave state, Maine entered as a free state, and slavery was prohibited in all new states formed from the portion of the Louisiana Purchase that lay north of the 36th parallel. Increasingly, there was little sense of unity within the Union.

The Great Triumvirate

Senators Daniel Webster of Massachusetts, Henry Clay of Kentucky and John C. Calhoun of South Carolina, left to right, dominated American politics for decades; working together to rise above sectionalism, they held the country together in the years after the Missouri Compromise. When their Compromise of 1850 unraveled, the nation was put on a course for Civil War.

33

Audubon's Wonderland

The son of a French sea captain and his mistress, John James Audubon was educated in France but immigrated to the U.S. in 1803, settling on a family farm in Pennsylvania. Artistic from early on and a lover of America's vast untrammeled spaces, he set out to explore the frontier, coming to rest in Kentucky. He traveled through the Mississippi River basin for the next two decades, working on his great project, the creation of an album of every species of bird then found in the U.S., stalking, shooting and stuffing the specimens he painted.

With the 1827 publication in England of his oversized, elegant volume *Birds of America*—which featured such limpid visions of the nation's birds and their Edenic habitats as this portrayal of reddish egrets *(Egretta rufescens)*—Audubon became world famous. Promoting himself as the "American Woodsman," he spent his later years painting the nation's mammals and other wildlife.

Andrew Jackson: War Hero, Frontiersman, President

In 1828, in one of the greatest sea-changes in U.S. political history, war hero Andrew Jackson became the first man of the frontier elected President. "Old Hickory" benefited from an expansion of suffrage (at least for white men) that abolished property requirements, increasing voter turnout some 130% over the 1824 tally. Jackson's military bearing and personal charisma made him one of the few figures in U.S. history to resemble Europe's iconic "man on horseback" (among others: George Washington, Teddy Roosevelt and Dwight Eisenhower).

Yet Jackson, at heart a bearer of frontier values, had none of Washington's aristocratic reserve: his Inauguration, below, turned into a tawdry bacchanal in which thousands of his unwashed followers rummaged through the White House, raiding buffet tables, wrecking fine furnishings and scandalizing proper Washington society. *Yee-haw!* America's Wild West had taken power in the East.

Native Americans Follow a Trail of Tears • 1838

Whites called Andrew Jackson "Old Hickory," but Native Americans used a more telling nickname: "Sharp Knife." In his military career, Jackson led several appallingly brutal campaigns against Creek and Seminole tribes in Mississippi and Florida. As President, Jackson approved a policy, euphemistically called "removal," that forced Eastern Indian tribes to move west of the Mississippi. (A generation later, the same tribes would be moved still farther west, once again at gunpoint.)

Jackson's hand-picked successor, Martin Van Buren, ordered the Cherokee Nation forced out of Georgia in 1838. Some 15,000 Cherokee left their homes and livestock and were ordered to march more than 800 miles westward during a severe winter; more than 4,000 died en route. The Cherokee called their trek into exile the Trail of Tears; the path they followed was designated a national monument in 1987.

Trail of Tears National Historic Trail: ••••Land Route ▬▬Water Route ▬▬Other Major Routes

As Immigration Swells, a Backlash Begins

Almost as soon as the smoke had cleared from the last shots fired in the War of 1812, the first of several great waves of immigrants (more than 5 million of them) began landing on American shores, primarily from England, Ireland and Germany. The newcomers sparked a "nativist" movement (a cruelly ironic name, given the tortured relations between the nation's first white immigrants and its authentic natives), aimed at keeping more foreigners out of the country and limiting the rights of those already present.

The tactics of anti-immigration militants ranged from manhandling newcomers to staging riots to forming political parties. The nativist activists, stimulated by cartoons like the one at left ridiculing Irish and German voters as corrupt drunkards, would coalesce into the Know-Nothing Party of the 1850s.

Acceleration, the Sensation of the Nation

Taming America's vast expanses required faster, more efficient ways of moving people and freight than by horse- and ox-drawn wagons. In the early 1800s, two innovations based on steam power, the steamboat and the railroad, began to speed up Uncle Sam's gait. In 1807 Robert Fulton's *Clermont*, above, made the round trip between New York City and Albany on the Hudson River in a record-breaking five days. In 1825 the Erie Canal across New York State opened, top: its 363-mile route linking New York City to the Great Lakes cut freight costs to the interior 95%. Americans were learning to shape the nation's landscape to fit their needs.

Railroads began to spread across the land in the 1820s, going where floating vessels could not: over mountains, through deserts, across swamps and into the nation's boundless interior. At right is a locomotive of Mississippi's Natchez & Hamburg Railroad line, circa 1836-38. By 1840, some 3,000 miles of rails united the states, at a time when all of Europe had fewer than 1,800 miles of track.

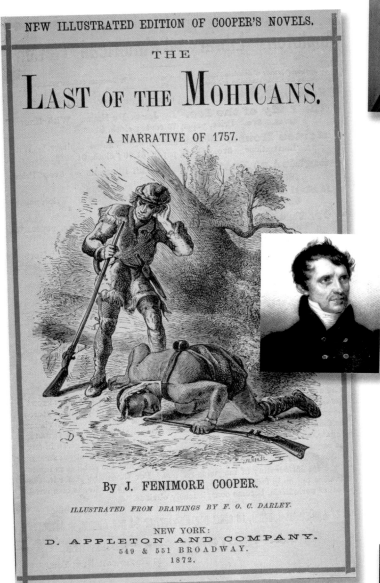

NEW ILLUSTRATED EDITION OF COOPER'S NOVELS.

THE
LAST OF THE MOHICANS.

A NARRATIVE OF 1757.

By J. FENIMORE COOPER.

ILLUSTRATED FROM DRAWINGS BY F. O. C. DARLEY.

NEW YORK:
D. APPLETON AND COMPANY.
549 & 551 BROADWAY.
1872.

Artists Explore and Shape the Nation's Heritage

In colonial times and through the revolutionary period, American writers and artists copied the styles and subjects of Europe's masters. But in the decades after independence, they began to embrace their homeland as their subject. Washington Irving, America's first true man of letters, began his career by satirizing New York City manners but struck a rich, romantic vein with his 1820 tales of Rip Van Winkle and Ichabod Crane. James Fenimore Cooper was the first writer to portray life on the frontier and probe the tensions between whites and Native Americans in his classic series of Leatherstocking novels, launched in 1823. Clergyman Clement C. Moore virtually invented secular Christmas lore in America with his beloved 1823 narrative poem, *A Visit from St. Nicholas.*

In the 1820s, painters of the Hudson River School began celebrating the sheer splendor of America's landscape. Asher Durand's *Kindred Spirits* (1849), left, shows artist Thomas Cole and poet William Cullen Bryant enjoying a spectacular view in the Catskill Mountains in New York State.

"(It is) ... our manifest destiny to overspread and to possess the whole of the continent which Providence has given us for the development of the great experiment of liberty."

—JOHN L. O'SULLIVAN, NEWSPAPER COLUMNIST, 1845

VINOTERIA

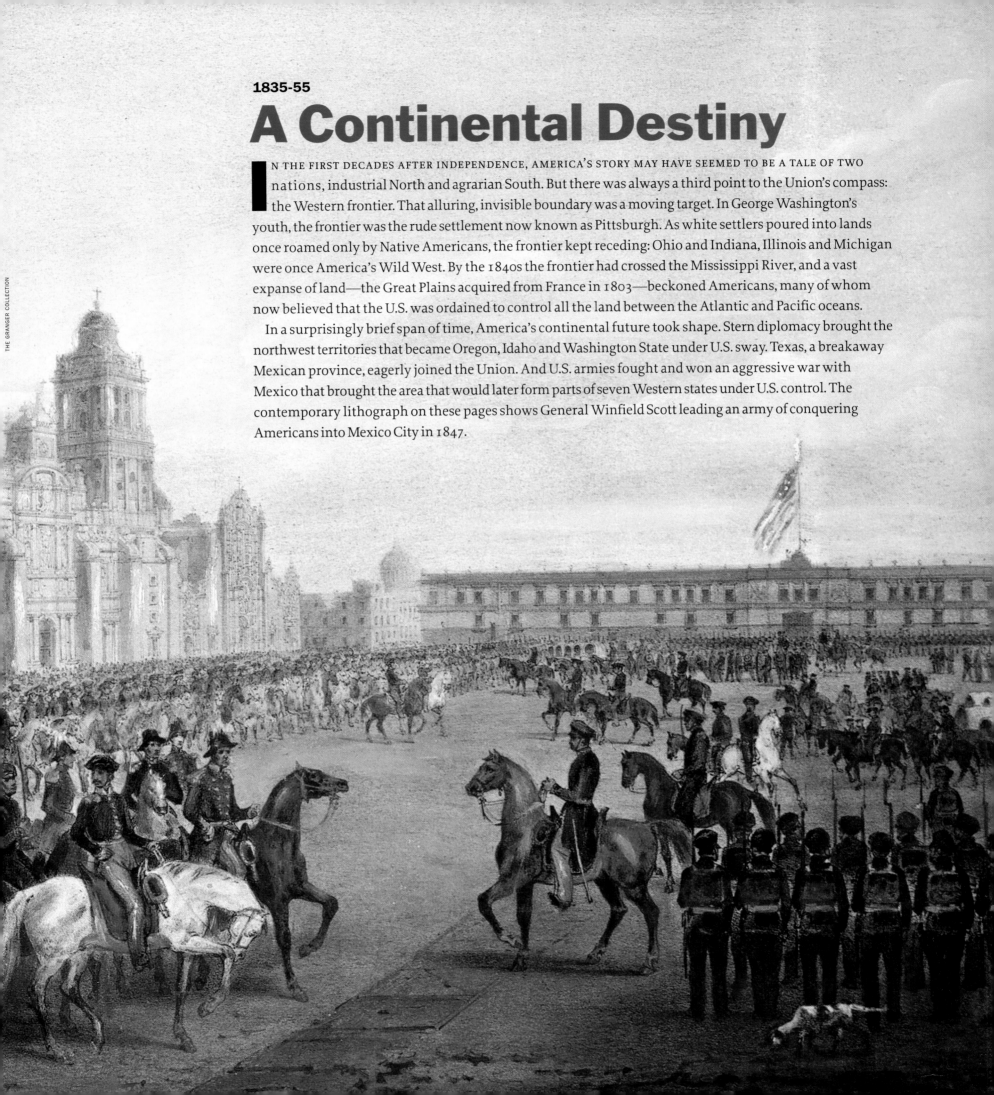

A Continental Destiny

I N THE FIRST DECADES AFTER INDEPENDENCE, AMERICA'S STORY MAY HAVE SEEMED TO BE A TALE OF TWO nations, industrial North and agrarian South. But there was always a third point to the Union's compass: the Western frontier. That alluring, invisible boundary was a moving target. In George Washington's youth, the frontier was the rude settlement now known as Pittsburgh. As white settlers poured into lands once roamed only by Native Americans, the frontier kept receding: Ohio and Indiana, Illinois and Michigan were once America's Wild West. By the 1840s the frontier had crossed the Mississippi River, and a vast expanse of land—the Great Plains acquired from France in 1803—beckoned Americans, many of whom now believed that the U.S. was ordained to control all the land between the Atlantic and Pacific oceans.

In a surprisingly brief span of time, America's continental future took shape. Stern diplomacy brought the northwest territories that became Oregon, Idaho and Washington State under U.S. sway. Texas, a breakaway Mexican province, eagerly joined the Union. And U.S. armies fought and won an aggressive war with Mexico that brought the area that would later form parts of seven Western states under U.S. control. The contemporary lithograph on these pages shows General Winfield Scott leading an army of conquering Americans into Mexico City in 1847.

JIM BOWIE

DAVY CROCKETT

SAM HOUSTON

Vol. 2.] "GO AHEAD!!" [No. 3.

THE CROCKETT ALMANAC
1841.

Containing Adventures, Exploits, Sprees
& Scrapes in the West, &
Life and Manners in the Backwoods.

Nashville, Tennessee. Published by Ben Harding.

A Frontier Legend

Among those who died at the Alamo
was the Tennessee frontiersman
Davy Crockett, who parlayed tall
tales of his backwoods adventures
into two terms in the U.S. House of
Representatives. Crockett's name
was still being used to sell almanacs
five years after his death, above.

Another legendary frontiersman
died in the Alamo: Kentucky-born
Jim Bowie, whose famous "Bowie
knife" sported a blade 10 in. long.

ANDRE JENNY—ALAMY

"Remember the Alamo!" • 1836

Early in the 19th century, a growing number
of Americans began settling in Texas, then a
northern province of Mexico. But the "Texians"
chafed under the rule of Hispanic Roman
Catholics and declared their independence in
1836. (One reason: Mexico freed its slaves in
1821, and most Texians had arrived from
Southern states.) Mexican strongman Antonio
López de Santa Anna soon invaded the breakaway Republic of Texas and surrounded the
Texians' stronghold in San Antonio, a small
Catholic mission known as "the Alamo," which
stood amid a grove of cottonwood trees, *alamos*
in Spanish. Some 187 frontiersmen barricaded
themselves within its walls, defying orders from
Republic of Texas leader Sam Houston to give
up the post. In a heroic siege that lasted 13 days,
the small band of Texians held off repeated
charges from some 5,000 Mexican troops.

On March 6, Santa Anna's artillery breached
the Alamo's walls and his troops rushed inside,
killing every soldier they found still alive, then
soaking their bodies with kerosene and setting
them aflame. A small group of women, children
and slaves were allowed to leave. Seven weeks
later, rallying under the cry "Remember the
Alamo!" Texian forces under Houston defeated
Santa Anna in the Battle of San Jacinto, took him
prisoner and chased his army back into Mexico.
The Texians voted to seek annexation by the
U.S. shortly after their victory, but their goal
would not be realized until 1845.

43

A "Dark Horse" Reshapes the Nation

President James K. Polk is little recalled by modern Americans—but he ought to be. The Tennessean, the original "dark horse" of U.S. politics (shown at right at the White House in 1849), was a surprise winner of the 1844 election; in his single term, the devout expansionist added more land to the U.S. than did Thomas Jefferson with the Louisiana Purchase.

Polk secured the Oregon Territory from Britain; the vast area later became the states of Oregon, Idaho and Washington. He waged a controversial war with Mexico that added 520,000 sq. mi. of land to the U.S., including all of California, Nevada and Utah and most of Arizona. He also brought Texas into the Union.

The Mexican War was the first major conflict in history to be photographed; above, U.S. Army cavalrymen ride through the streets of Saltillo, circa 1847.

"Manifest Destiny" Brings a War with Mexico • 1846-47

America in the 1840s was a rawboned, rambunctious nation, still occupied with the business of settling a frontier—and deeply concerned that there be more frontier to settle. Newspaperman John L. O'Sullivan caught the spirit of the times when he declared in 1845 that it was the nation's "manifest destiny" to spread from the Atlantic to the Pacific. His phrase became the rallying cry of expansionists, who craved vast tracts of land in the West for the Union—and, perhaps, for potential profits.

Among the most fervent of the expansionists was President Polk: when his attempts to purchase land from Mexico failed, he trumped up a case for war and sent armies under generals Winfield Scott and Zachary Taylor to Mexico. Scott, above, landed at Veracruz in the first large-scale amphibious invasion in U.S. history, below, then easily occupied Mexico City. In the Mexican Cession that followed, Mexico's size shrank almost 40%, while the size of the U.S. increased some 33%.

Rehearsal for a Civil War

Many of the U.S. Army officers who would later fight in the Civil War served in Mexico. Some 13,000 U.S. soldiers died in the campaign, the vast majority from disease rather than enemy fire.

45

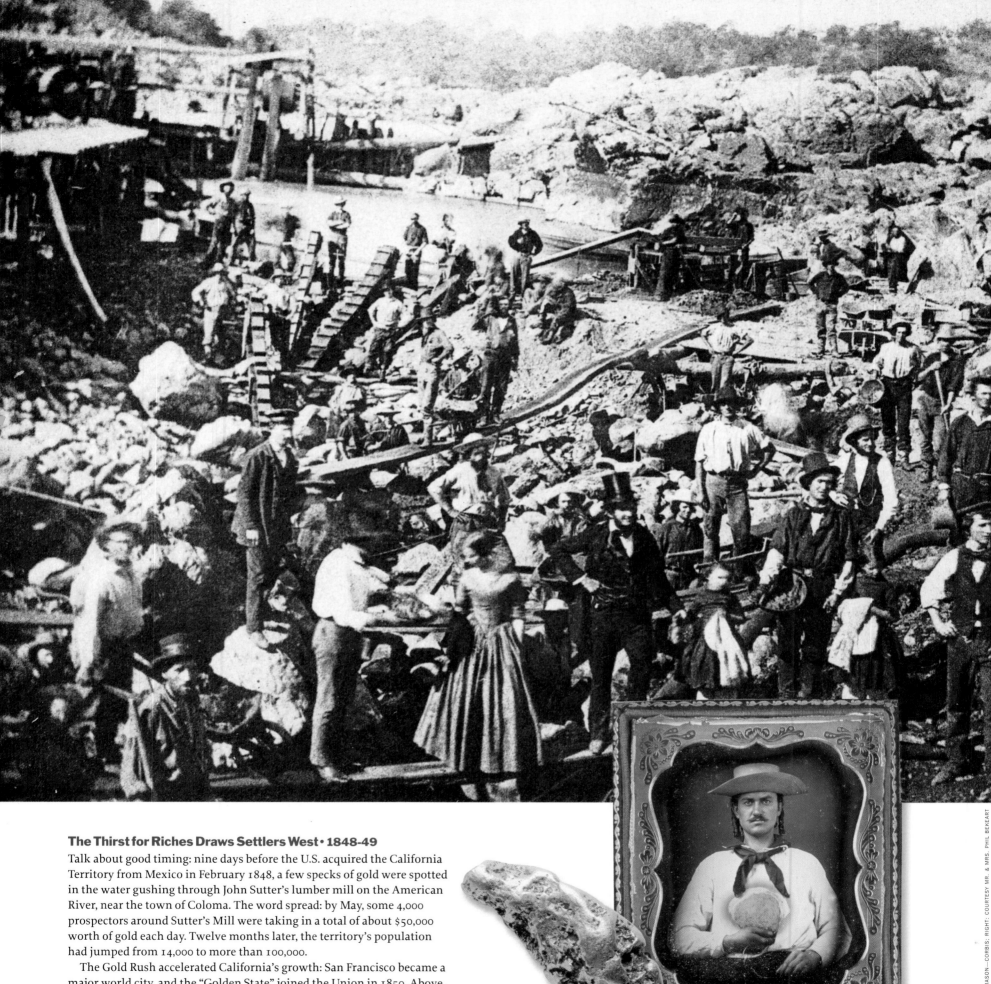

The Thirst for Riches Draws Settlers West • 1848-49

Talk about good timing: nine days before the U.S. acquired the California Territory from Mexico in February 1848, a few specks of gold were spotted in the water gushing through John Sutter's lumber mill on the American River, near the town of Coloma. The word spread: by May, some 4,000 prospectors around Sutter's Mill were taking in a total of about $50,000 worth of gold each day. Twelve months later, the territory's population had jumped from 14,000 to more than 100,000.

The Gold Rush accelerated California's growth: San Francisco became a major world city, and the "Golden State" joined the Union in 1850. Above, prospectors (and a few friends) pose for a portrait in 1849 in the American River Basin; at right, a Forty-Niner shows off his find the same year.

LEFT: DON MASON—CORBIS; RIGHT: COURTESY MR. & MRS. PHIL BEKEART

LEFT: GEORGE DOYLE—GETTY IMAGES; RIGHT: THE GRANGER COLLECTION

Rise and Fall of the California Republic • 1846

The U.S. acquired California as a result of its 1848 victory in the Mexican War. But two years earlier, English-speaking settlers had tried to jump-start this process. Stirred up by celebrated explorer and U.S. Army Captain John C. Frémont, right, they declared their independence from Mexico in June 1846, creating the California Republic. Oops! The slow-traveling news hadn't reached them: Washington had declared war on Mexico the previous month. The settlers dropped their pretension to autonomy, began fighting under the American flag and worked to make California part of the Union.

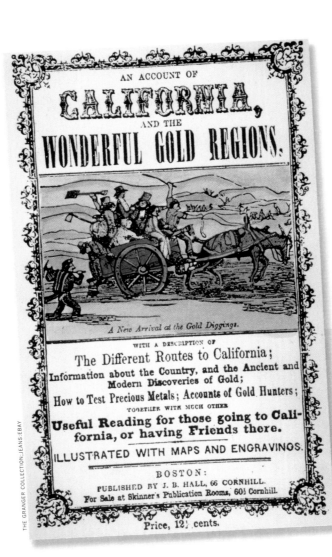

THE GRANGER COLLECTION/JEANS: EBAY

CARLTON E. WATKINS

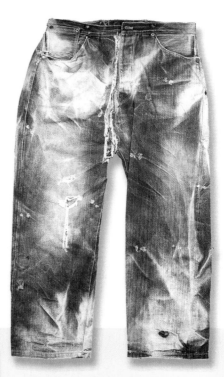

Blue Trousers, Golden Dreams

New York merchant Levi Strauss went west to sell tents in 1853, but miners preferred his rugged pants, made from serge woven in Nimes, France. "Serge de Nimes" soon became "denim"—and Americans had found the "Levi's" that remain their national uniform and emblem. Above is the oldest known pair, which sold for $46,500 on eBay in 2003. At left, a book hawks California's gold fields.

48

Women Call for Equal Rights • 1848

In an age of new technologies and new frontiers, American women were locked into old social roles—marriage or teaching was their assigned destiny—and a few of them began to share their frustrations. Led by Elizabeth Cady Stanton, right, Lucretia Mott and others, a group of like-minded women gathered at the Seneca Falls Convention in New York State in July 1848, above, and issued a call for increased women's rights based on the ideas stated in the Declaration of Independence. Believing that the elaborate clothing of the time helped restrict women's lives, suffragist Amelia Jenks Bloomer introduced loose trousers to be worn under the era's long skirts, far right, to permit freedom of movement.

The Seneca Falls gathering was initially ignored and women's "Bloomers" were scorned, but a movement for change had been established. Even so, it was not until 1920, 72 years after the convention, that U.S. women were enfranchised.

Weaving New Lives from New Technologies

As the Industrial Revolution began remaking American society, employers needed capable, reliable workers. In Lowell, Mass., center, home to the nation's first large-scale textile factories, owners began hiring young women to work the looms. The "factory girls" lived in owner-provided, supervised dormitories and published a literary magazine, the *Lowell Offering*. Their lives amounted to a quiet revolution.

49

A Continental Destiny

Strong New Voices Explore America's Inner Frontiers

John Adams famously declared he "must study politics and war [so] that my sons may have liberty to study mathematics and philosophy … in order to give their children a right to study painting, poetry, music, architecture …" Adams' vision arrived right on time, as America, long scorned by Europeans as a cultural backwater, flourished in the late 1840s and early '50s with the work of a magnificent generation of artists.

New England public intellectuals Ralph Waldo Emerson and Henry David Thoreau celebrated nature and explored the role of the individual in society, while a very private intellectual, Emily Dickinson, created searing poems that have far outlasted their time. Nathaniel Hawthorne probed America's Puritan inheritance in his memorable, influential novels and short stories.

Herman Melville and Edgar Allan Poe pursued personal visions; Melville launched his career with journalistic yarns of his travels in the South Seas as a sailor, then moved on to create epic allegories of American life, including the classic novel *Moby-Dick*. Poe, a gifted poet and the lone Southerner in this literary pantheon, was a pioneer of literary formats, creating the modern detective story and the short, morbid tale of terror.

One artist most deeply caught the timbres of America's national voice— its "barbaric yawp"—and its restless, optimistic spirit: New York poet Walt Whitman. In *Leaves of Grass* (1855), Whitman became the pathfinder of U.S. literature, breaking the ground of direct, unblinking personal expression that would be tilled by thousands of American writers to come.

WALT WHITMAN

In Tune with His Times

Prospectors headed west in the Gold Rush to the supremely catchy tune of *Oh! Susanna*, the song Stephen Foster biographer Ken Emerson called "a new national anthem." The Pittsburgh-born Foster may be the nation's greatest songwriter; such classic works as *Oh! Susanna, Camptown Races* and *Old Folks at Home* still touch the mystic chords of memory in American hearts.

Sadly, some of Foster's songs were written in the minstrel idiom and reflect the casual, deeply embedded racism of mainstream American culture in his time. Here is *Oh! Susanna's* seldom-heard second stanza, in its original spelling:

I jump'd aboard the telegraph and trabbled down de ribber
De lectrick fluid magnified and kill'd five hundred Nigga.
De bulgine bust and de hoss ran off, I really thought I'd die
I shut my eyes to hold my bref, Susanna don't you cry.

RALPH WALDO EMERSON

HENRY DAVID THOREAU

EMILY DICKINSON

EDGAR ALLAN POE

HERMAN MELVILLE

NATHANIEL HAWTHORNE

51

"They had for more than a century before been regarded as beings of an inferior order, and altogether unfit to associate with the white race, either in social or political relations, and so far inferior that they had no rights which the white man was bound to respect."

—ROGER B. TANEY, CHIEF JUSTICE OF THE U.S. SUPREME COURT, *DRED SCOTT v. SANDFORD, 1857*

The Bondsman's Toil

SLAVERY IS OLD IN AMERICA, OLDER BY FAR THAN THE U.S.: 20 AFRICAN SLAVES LANDED IN VIRGINIA IN 1619, 157 years before the slaveholder Thomas Jefferson wrote a ringing reveille in the Declaration of Independence: "We hold these truths to be self-evident, that all men are created equal..." Aiming to reconcile the nation's gleaming ideals with its squalid realities, all the states in the North, where the economy was not based on slave-tended plantation crops, had outlawed the practice of keeping human chattels by 1804. But Southerners defended the "peculiar institution," arguing that slaves were private property and thus protected by law. Three great compromises—in 1790, 1820 and 1850— were crafted to hold the Union together; the price was the preservation of slavery in the South. By 1850, 1 in every 8 Americans was a black slave, and the struggle over what Abraham Lincoln called "the bondsman's 250 years of unrequited toil" was straining the nation's unity, shredding its civility, challenging its laws and mocking its founding principles.

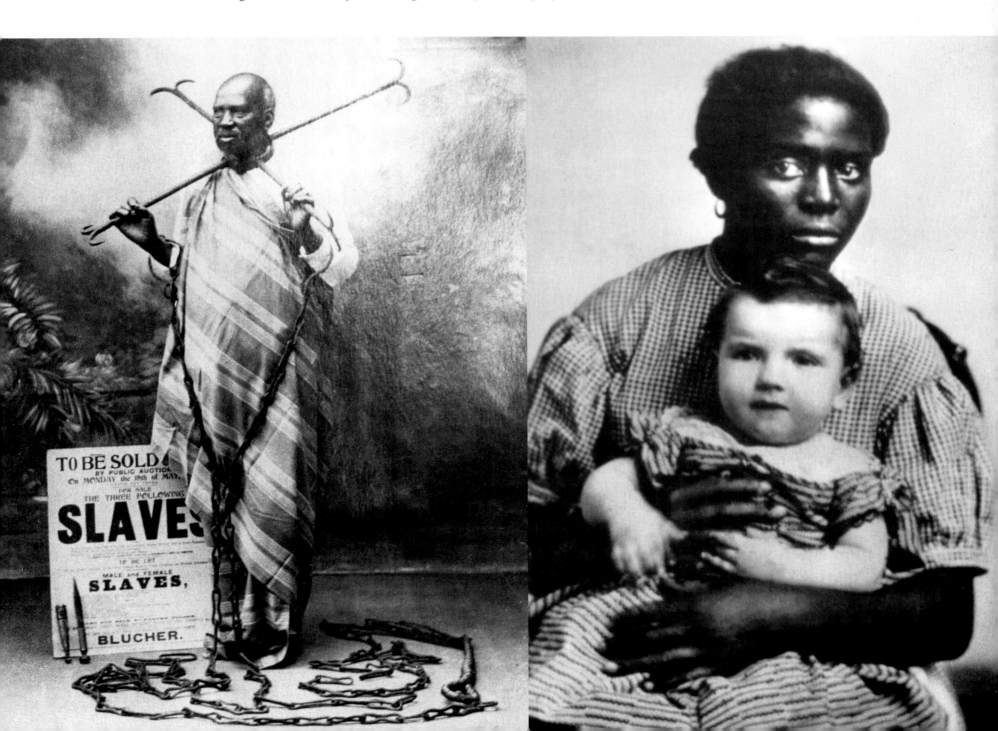

Journey into Bondage

Most slaves were brought into the U.S. by the harrowing overseas route mariners called "the middle passage" across the Atlantic, in a triangle of trade involving three primary commodities: slaves from Africa, crops and raw materials from the Americas and manufactured goods from Europe.

Aboard the ships, as many as 400 to 700 slaves were shackled together belowdecks, as shown at right; in the unsanitary conditions, disease, hunger and depression claimed the lives of an estimated 50% of those who began the journey. Once in the U.S. and put up for sale at auction houses like the one pictured at far right in Alexandria, Va., slaves, as chattels, had no rights, and families were often separated.

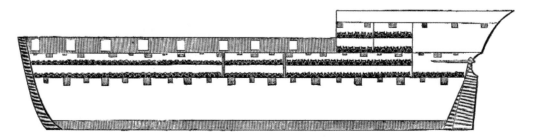

Scars and Stripes

As the Northern states increasingly came to see slavery as a moral evil, the importation of slaves into the U.S. was outlawed in 1808, when some 1 million slaves lived in the U.S. But that did not put an end to slavery's growth: at the beginning of the Civil War, the slave population had risen to 4 million. While slavery was founded on racism, sexual relationships between white owners and black slave women were widespread.

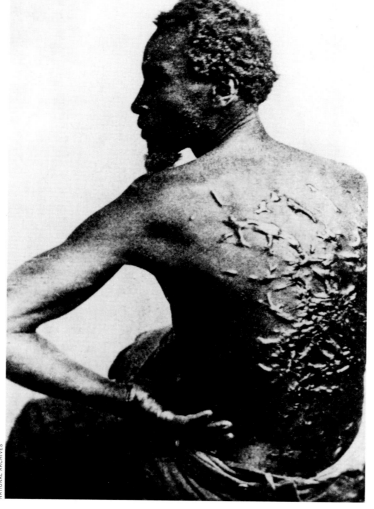

NATIONAL ARCHIVES

It is impossible to generalize about the daily lives of slaves. Some of them were brutalized by the whip, like Peter, above, freed by Union troops and photographed in Baton Rouge, La., in 1863, who said he was "two months in bed sore from the whipping," while others were treated with (relatively) more decency. As the Southern plantation system evolved, slave society became divided between more polished house slaves, who served as domestics in plantation homes, and field hands, like the family pictured at left outside Savannah, Ga., in the 1860s.

SMITHSONIAN INSTITUTION

55

Symbol of Servitude

Slaveholders used a variety of techniques to break the will of any slave who resisted bondage, including the forced wearing of iron neck hoops. Aristocratic owners often consigned the treatment of their unpaid laborers to middlemen, the brutal slave drivers.

NATIONAL ARCHIVES

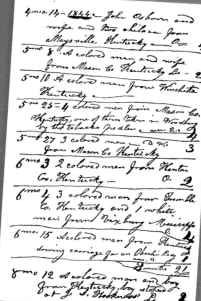

Slaves' Deliverance: The Underground Railroad

If modern accounts of the successes of the Underground Railroad are a bit overblown, the electrifying effect of this clandestine escape system—both on slaves thirsting for freedom and abolitionists working to aid them—cannot be overstated. The Railroad, operated by a loose network of antislavery activists, sheltered runaway slaves in free states adjacent to Southern states and ferried them to New England or Canada. It helped free thousands of African Americans from bondage (the exact number is unknown, although credible estimates run to higher than 10,000).

The 19th century map above traces Railroad routes in southeastern Pennsylvania; the ledger page beside it records runaway slaves who passed through an Ohio home linked to the system in 1844. The "slave pen" below, in Mason County, Ky., held fugitives and slaves waiting to be sold. Quilts like the one at right are said to be coded maps showing escape routes, but some scholars reject such claims. The secret crawl space shown on the far right was built into the residence of an abolitionist Protestant minister in Pennsylvania.

SLAVERY'S FOES

The battle to abolish slavery as an immoral and corrupt practice was strongest in New England, where ministers and activists denounced it for decades. But no person or event created as much sympathy for the slaves and hatred of the "peculiar institution" as a single novel, Harriet Beecher Stowe's mammoth 1852 best seller, *Uncle Tom's Cabin,* often described as the book that lit the flames of Civil War

135,000 SETS, 270,000 VOLUMES SOLD.

UNCLE TOM'S CABIN

FOR SALE HERE.

AN EDITION FOR THE MILLION, COMPLETE IN 1 Vol., PRICE 37 1-2 CENTS.
" " IN GERMAN, IN 1 Vol. PRICE 50 CENTS.
" " IN 2 Vols. CLOTH, 6 PLATES, PRICE $1.50.
SUPERB ILLUSTRATED EDITION, IN 1 Vol. WITH 153 ENGRAVINGS.
PRICES FROM $2.50 TO $5.00.

The Greatest Book of the Age.

Warriors for Freedom

In the 1850s the battles over slavery flared to new heights, as abolitionists accelerated their attempts to ban the institution. Harriet Tubman, top left, an escaped Maryland slave, helped more than 70 slaves reach freedom. Militant John Brown, top center, fought slaveholders in Kansas, then raided a Virginia armory in hopes of starting an insurrection; he was hanged in 1859.

Uncle Tom's Cabin, which demonized those who owned slaves, was America's best-selling 19th century novel. Sojourner Truth, above, was a pioneering feminist and abolitionist. Frederick Douglass, shown at right in 1850, was the most respected black American of his time; he argued eloquently and effectively against slavery.

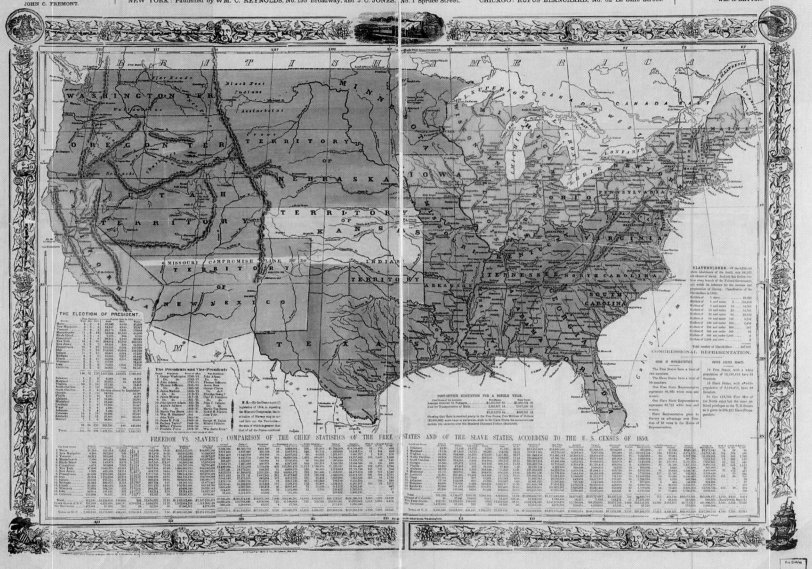

58

Cartography of a Crisis

The 1854 map above charts the deep divisions of the Union in the decade before the Civil War. States where slavery was legal are brown; those where slavery was outlawed appear in red. Grey areas are territories under U.S. control that have not yet become states. Under the controversial Compromise of 1850, California joined the Union as a free state, slavery was not outlawed in the New Mexico Territory, and a tough new Fugitive Slave Law was passed.

As a result of the Compromise, tensions mounted over whether new states carved out of the Western territories would be slave or free. Under Illinois Senator Stephen Douglas' Kansas-Nebraska Act of 1854, settlers in these new states would decide by popular vote whether slavery would be legal. The law led to guerrilla warfare in the territory of "Bleeding Kansas," right, where pro- and anti-slavery forces battled in the streets to control the future.

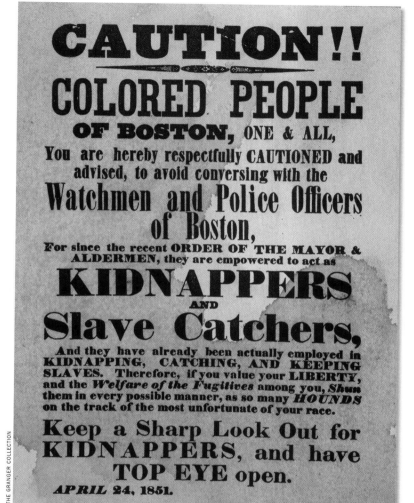

Dred Scott and the Fugitive Slave Act • 1850

The Compromise of 1850 strengthened the Fugitive Slave Law, leading to posters like the one at right in fiercely abolitionist Massachusetts. It also spawned a pivotal event, the divisive *Dred Scott* case, in which Scott, a slave, argued that he and his wife, above, ought to be free, since their owner had transported them to Illinois, a free state.

The U.S. Supreme Court disagreed in 1857, ruling, in essence, that all African Americans were "beings of an inferior order" who could never become citizens of the U.S. and holding that the 1820 Missouri Compromise, which outlawed slavery north of the 36th parallel, was invalid. The decision ignited the nation: foes of slavery feared it might become legal in every state, while Southern voices began calling for outright secession from the Union.

59

The Minstrel Show's Enduring Legacy

A complex, racist and peculiarly American art form, the minstrel show originated in the 1830s as a hybrid of music, dance and comedy based on the revels of African-American slaves. The form trafficked in outlandish racial stereotypes—yet the vitality of its banjo-driven music and dances swept the nation. The minstrel show, vaudeville's precursor, was the most popular form of live entertainment in the U.S. in the 19th century, whether performed by blacks or by its original practitioners, white entertainers whose faces were blackened by cork.

The radio comedy *Amos 'n' Andy,* which featured two white men lampooning black dialect, played well into the 1950s on national radio networks. Private white social groups performed blackface minstrel shows as recently as the 1960s in the South and Midwest. In more recent times, critics have charged black rap performers who trade in exaggerated racial personas with practicing a form of demeaning, updated minstrelsy.

Spike Lee's 2000 film *Bamboozled* is a rare modern effort to explore the effects of the minstrel show on American society. The outdated form, though an essential thread in U.S. cultural history, remains such a racially charged subject that it has now become a taboo, deliberately ignored aspect of the past.

84th REG'T
U.S. Colored Infantry.
Port Hudson La July 1863
Pleasant Hill La April 1864
Mansura La May 1864
Bayou De Glaise La
White Ranche Texas

FLAG: SMITHSONIAN INSTITUTION—CORBIS; DRUM: TRIA GIOVAN—CORBIS

1860-65

Crisis of the Union

America's great experiment with freedom and liberty seemed an utter failure by 1860, as northern and Southern states battled over the ethics and politics of human slavery. The nation's founding documents promised that all men were created equal; the practice of slavery mocked that vision. The reckoning between ideals and realities had been building for more than 80 years: now it was at hand. Yet no one dreamed just how bloody and uncivil this war between the states would become. The Civil War is a watershed in America's history, the cleansing moment that consigned slavery to the past—yet even so, it did not end the nation's sectional divisions or win full rights for African Americans. Above is a battle flag of the 84th Regiment, U.S. Colored Infantry, a black Union cadre; opposite page, the battle flag of the 4th Virginia Infantry.

"Both parties deprecated war; but one of them would make war rather than let the nation survive; and the other would accept war rather than let it perish. And the war came."

—ABRAHAM LINCOLN, SECOND INAUGURAL ADDRESS, 1865

The Rise of Abraham Lincoln

Born in a cabin on the Kentucky frontier in 1809, Abraham Lincoln was largely self-educated; he worked as a boathand and storekeeper before becoming a successful lawyer in Springfield, Ill., where he married the well-to-do Mary Todd, below, in 1842. Elected to the U.S. House of Representatives in 1846, he opposed and denounced the popular war with Mexico and did not run for re-election.

Opposed to the spread of slavery, the homely, eloquent Lincoln joined the new Republican Party and ran against Stephen A. Douglas for the U.S. Senate in 1858. Lincoln lost, but his brilliance in their celebrated debates brought him national attention—and the Republican Party's nomination for the presidency in 1860. Declaring the Union could not survive as "a house divided," he was elected. The 1846 portrait at left above is the earliest photograph of Lincoln; the others are from 1860 and 1865.

Lincoln Election Materials

Lincoln, only the second Republican to run for the presidency, campaigned with Maine Senator Hannibal Hamlin in 1860, beating three other candidates. In 1864 his opponent was the Union general he fired in 1862, George B. McClellan.

Lincoln Takes Office but Presides over a Shattered Union

Even before Lincoln was inaugurated on March 4, 1861, seven states—South Carolina, Mississippi, Florida, Alabama, Georgia, Louisiana and Texas—declared they would secede from the Union to form the Confederate States of America. After the first shots of the Civil War were fired at Fort Sumter in South Carolina on April 12, 1861, four more states joined the Confederacy: Virginia, Arkansas, Tennessee and North Carolina. Missouri and Kentucky were frontier "border states," where slavery was legal, though far less pervasive than in the plantation-economy states of the deep South. Confederate rump governments were formed in each state, but the Union controlled both border states during the war.

In his role as Commander in Chief of the U.S. Army, Lincoln was hard-pressed to find military leadership that could marshal the North's overwhelming advantage in manpower, resources and industry to defeat the well-led Southern armies. Above, Lincoln poses with security chief Allan Pinkerton, left, and General John A. McClernand on Oct. 3, 1862, two weeks after the bloody Battle of Antietam in Maryland.

First Shots: Fort Sumter • 1861

The war that would kill more Americans than any other U.S. conflict began with a battle that took not a single life. The flashpoint was the federal armory at Fort Sumter, in the Charleston, S.C., harbor. At 4:30 a.m. on April 12, 1861, some five weeks after Abraham Lincoln took the oath of office in a drastically diminished Union, Confederate General Pierre Beauregard began shelling the fort. Some 34 hours later, Union Major Robert Anderson (who had been Beauregard's teacher at West Point) surrendered.

In a deceptively benign start to what would become a long and grisly war, Beauregard graciously allowed the Yankees safe conduct back to Union territory. Left, a contemporary illustration of Confederate artillery shelling the fort; above, Union troops strike a pose after Fort Sumter was retaken by the North in 1863.

THE GRANGER COLLECTION

CORBIS

A First Encounter's "Great Skedaddle" • 1861

The bloodless Battle of Fort Sumter fed hopes, especially in the North, that the secession crisis was more dramatic than deadly. So fashionable Washingtonians packed lunches and picnicked on hillsides near Bull Run Creek in Manassas, Va., on July 21, 1861, after newspapers published the time and place where, they explained, numerically superior Union forces would meet the upstart Southern troops and put an end to the rebellion.

Confederate generals Pierre Beauregard and Thomas (Stonewall) Jackson didn't read the newspapers: after some early setbacks, they sent the Union's green troops—and their stunned admirers—reeling back to the capital in a hasty retreat that crowing Southerners quickly dubbed "the great skedaddle."

Above, children eye cavalrymen at a ford near the battlefield; at right, a contemporary sketch of the battle.

Backstage, Fiddles and Morphine

Although such generals as Ulysses S. Grant and Robert E. Lee commanded well-trained, well-equipped armies (until the South's resources were exhausted), many units that served in the Civil War were little more than ragtag bands of state militiamen who might appear for duty after the spring crops were planted, sporting mismatched uniforms and scant knowledge of military tactics. The colleagues above, part of a company of Confederate soldiers from Louisiana, seem as prepared for a drinking party as for a battle.

Behind the scenes, tens of thousands of women on both sides of the fray served as nurses in camp hospitals. At right, federal nurse Anne Bell tends to Northern troops. In the days before antibiotics, thousands of wounded soldiers succumbed to infection.

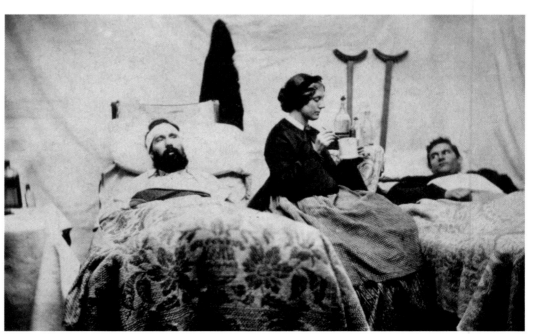

YANKEE AND REBEL, YOUNG AND OLD, BLACK AND WHITE, SUNDERED AMERICANS GO TO WAR

The largest war ever fought on U.S. soil completely absorbed the nation; boys as young as 12 donned uniforms to fight for the Union or the Confederacy, although the uniforms they wore often varied from the standard blue and grey of the more organized armies

Faces of the Warriors

Soldiers marching off to war frequently sat for a last portrait. Many such photos survive, but the names of those pictured have often been lost. At top left is a Union cavalryman in 1864. At top center is the Confederate Private Edwin E. Jemison, who enlisted at 16 in the 2nd Louisiana Regiment; he was killed at the Battle of Malvern Hill in Virginia in 1862.

Paymaster M. Howland of the 7th New York State Militia is at top right. The two Confederate soldiers at right may be brothers, since they were photographed together; their names are not known. Above is "Drummer" Jackson, a young former slave who served with Northern troops.

JAMES F. GIBSON—LIBRARY OF CONGRESS PRINTS AND PHOTOGRAPHS DIVISION

Battle of the Ironclads • 1862

The ironclad fighting ship was one of the key military innovations of the Civil War. The March 1862 Battle of Hampton Roads, off the Virginia coast, was the world's first engagement between two such ships, the U.S.S. *Monitor* and the C.S.S. *Virginia*. The *Monitor* carried the day, but the top-heavy ship later sank in a storm. Her remains were discovered in 1973. In 2003 her revolving gun turret, clearly visible in the 1862 picture at left, was raised from the sea floor.

A Northern Army Is Routed at Fredericksburg • 1862

President Lincoln was plagued by generals who either would not fight (such as George B. McClellan) or could not win. The incompetent Ambrose Burnside, McClellan's successor, was one of the latter; trying to take Fredericksburg, Va., in December 1862, he sent six waves of Union troops across an open field covered by Confederate riflemen and artillery. In a lopsided Southern victory, 12,000-plus Union troops were killed or wounded, twice the number of Confederate casualties. Below, Union troops view Southern positions after the battle.

68

MEDFORD HISTORICAL SOCIETY

Slaves Inch Closer to Freedom • 1862

The status of the South's slaves presented an ongoing crisis for both sides during the war; the Confiscation Act of 1862 freed slaves in Southern territory captured by Union forces and allowed them to serve in Union armies. Once news of the law spread, many slaves in Confederate territory began trying to make their way toward Union lines, lured by the promise of freedom. Above, a group of slaves crosses Virginia's Rappahannock River in August 1862, bound for Union ground.

King Cotton to the Defense • 1862

At right, Southern defenders at Yorktown, Va.—scene of the final British defeat in the Revolutionary War—use bales of cotton as fortifications when Union troops are besieging them in the spring of 1862. Cotton was the primary crop of the South, the pillar of the plantation economy—and a dandy barricade.

The savvy Confederates, feigning to have more men and armor than they actually commanded at Yorktown, tied down Union troops for weeks in the siege, then fled to fight another day.

A New Military Technology Takes Spycraft Up, Up and Away

When Abraham Lincoln read the words "I have the pleasure of sending you this first dispatch ever telegraphed from an aerial station," he was sold. On the evening of June 11, 1861, self-styled aeronaut Thaddeus Lowe had arranged for a demonstration of a new technology that he believed could be of great military value in the Civil War, then just two months old. In a basket tethered to the bottom of a hydrogen-filled balloon and equipped with telegraph gear, Lowe ascended to 500 ft. above the White House lawn and cabled back to the amazed President a description of everything he saw for miles around.

In October Lowe was named civilian chief of the new Union Army Balloon Corps. The Civil War was the first conflict in which air power played a role. But since the Union balloons remained tethered in one place due to the telegraph wires that relayed their information, they offered only the power to peer at the enemy, rather than shoot at him. Above, Lowe ascends in the balloon *Intrepid* during the Battle of Seven Pines in Virginia in May 1862, where his information saved a large number of Union troops from a Confederate trap. The Balloon Corps was disbanded in 1863 when Lowe resigned in a dispute over his pay.

The Gang's All Here: Camp Followers and Immigrants in the Civil War

A soldier from the 31st Pennsylvania Infantry Regiment poses with his wife and three children in 1862 in Washington. Throughout the Civil War, armies on both sides were often accompanied by a large contingent of families, provision suppliers, craftsmen and hangers-on. Many newly arrived immigrants served in the war, including an estimated 150,000 Irish-American soldiers, 75% of whom fought for the Union. Most served in segregated, Irish-only units like New York's "Fighting 69th," in part because recent waves of immigration from Catholic Europe had aroused considerable hostility among Protestant American "nativists," and in part because the Irish preferred it that way. Other newcomers also served: New York's 39th Infantry, composed mostly of recent Italian immigrants, called itself the Garibaldi Guard.

The largest contingent of minority soldiers in the war was a people whose ancestors crossed an ocean to come to America but had no choice in the matter. Some 180,000 African Americans (mostly free blacks, but some former slaves) fought on the Union side during the Civil War; a small number of slaves even fought for the South.

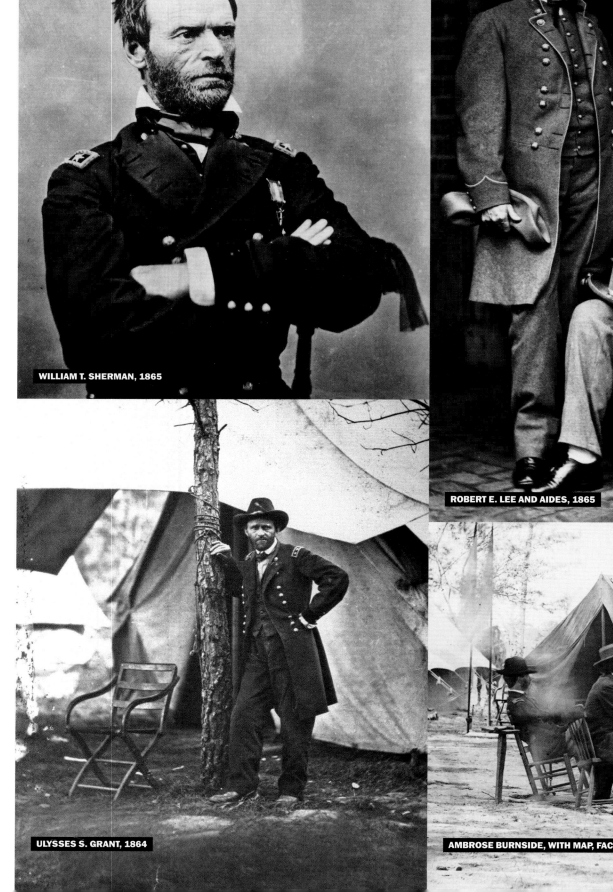

WILLIAM T. SHERMAN, 1865

ULYSSES S. GRANT, 1864

ROBERT E. LEE AND AIDES, 1865

AMBROSE BURNSIDE, WITH MAP, FACING PHOTOGRAPHER MATHEW BRADY, 1862

ULYSSES S. GRANT, LEFT, BENDING OVER MAP, 1864

GEORGE B. McCLELLAN, 1861

Comrades, Brothers, Enemies

Just as it sundered the Union, the war drove fissures through the officer corps of the U.S. Army, making foes of men who had graduated together from West Point and fought side by side in the Mexican War. If the Union boasted a larger population and stronger industrial base, the Confederacy countered with superior military leadership. Under commanders like Thomas (Stonewall) Jackson and Robert E. Lee (who, ironically, was no friend of slavery and opposed both secession and the war), Southern forces time and again produced victories against lopsided odds.

In contrast, Northern troops suffered—and were slaughtered—under the leadership of inept officers like George B. McClellan and Ambrose Burnside until Abraham Lincoln found the tough, hard-driving campaigners Ulysses S. Grant and William T. Sherman, who hammered out victory.

THOMAS (STONEWALL) JACKSON, 1863

74

The Bloodiest Single Day on American Soil: Slaughter at Antietam • 1862

Buoyed by his victory in routing Union General John Pope's Army of Virginia in the Second Battle of Bull Run in late August 1862, Confederate General Robert E. Lee led his Army of Northern Virginia into Maryland the next month, heading for Washington. In response, General George B. McClellan, the vainglorious, overly cautious leader of the Army of the Potomac, finally heeded Abraham Lincoln's pleas and sent his troops into battle.

Yet even though McClellan learned the details of Lee's battle plan in advance through a stroke of luck, his attack was timid and poorly coordinated. The result was a confused, day-long encounter that became a bloodbath; the "butcher's bill" numbered more than 10,000 Southern casualties, including some 1,500 dead, and an estimated 12,000 Northern casualties, including 2,000 dead. At right, fallen Southern soldiers lie along the Hagerstown Turnpike that divided the battlefield.

The battle was a strategic victory for the North, as Lee was forced to withdraw his army. Yet despite his overwhelming superiority in numbers and Lincoln's repeated urging, McClellan did not pursue Lee's battered army, and Lincoln relieved him of his command in November. Even so, the successful defense of Washington gave Lincoln the opening he needed to direct a political thrust at the South. Five days after the battle, he issued the Emancipation Proclamation, declaring that all slaves in seceded Southern states would be free as of Jan. 1, 1863—at once making the abolition of slavery a new goal of the war and helping undermine the Confederacy's slave-supported economy.

Visions of War As Never Seen Before

The Civil War burned itself into Americans' psyches not only because it divided families but also because it was the first war to be documented by the relatively new technology of photography. As recorded in all its grisly detail by pioneering photojournalists like Mathew Brady (with beard, above, in Virginia) and his associates, including Alexander Gardner and Timothy H. O'Sullivan, the cost of combat became vividly real for noncombatants as never before.

Because photography was still in its infancy, requiring long exposure times, Civil War pictures often portray soldiers posing before going into battle or lying dead in its wake, as in Gardner's famous photo of a fallen sharpshooter at "Devil's Den" in Gettysburg, below. Said Brady, in words that continue to influence photojournalists: "From the first, I regarded myself as under obligation to my country to preserve the faces of its historic men and mothers."

The War's Greatest Battle—and its Memorable Aftermath · 1863

The most significant battle of the Civil War began when an advance column of rebel troops invading Maryland and Pennsylvania stumbled onto a Union position outside the crossroads town of Gettysburg, Pa., on July 1, 1863. By the end of the next day, the brilliant Southern General Robert E. Lee had nearly completed a double envelopment of the Union forces. But on July 3, Lee blundered, sending a division of more than 15,000 men under Major General George Pickett in a direct charge against Union lines on the high ground of Cemetery Ridge. Pickett's Charge, if one of the most valiant actions in U.S. military history, left more than 10,000 rebels killed or wounded. Hoping to overcome the disaster, two more Southern divisions followed Pickett's lead and were also cut to pieces. When the three-day battle was over, more than 36,000 Americans were dead, wounded, missing or captured.

One day later and some 900 miles away, Union General Ulysses S. Grant captured the Confederate stronghold at Vicksburg, Miss., handing control of the Mississippi River to the Union. The twin victories were the war's decisive moment: the Union, clearly stronger in men and arms than the rebels, was not to be denied victory.

President Abraham Lincoln, seen above in the only picture that shows him at Gettysburg, delivered a memorial address on Nov. 19, 1863, in which he called on Americans to rededicate themselves to the nation's founding ideals and portrayed the war as a great test of whether a nation "conceived in Liberty and dedicated to the proposition that all men are created equal" could long endure.

Two Minutes That Changed a Nation

Lincoln spoke for less than two minutes at Gettysburg, yet his message renewed America's ideals. This manuscript in his hand, one of five that exist, includes only 10 sentences and 272 words. The legend persists that Lincoln wrote this profound document in haste on the train to the battlefield; in reality, he carefully revised his remarks in advance, as was his custom all his life.

78

A Vanquished South Agrees to Surrender • 1865

The last 12 months of the Civil War brought destruction on a scale never before seen in human conflict. Union top commander Ulysses S. Grant, the tough general Lincoln had been seeking for so long, believed that chewing up Southern troops in battle and torching Southern resources behind the lines was the only way to end the conflict.

Grant's first strategy cost the Union more than 66,000 casualties in just six weeks in the fall of 1864, but it inflicted even heavier losses on the South, now out of manpower and almost out of vital supplies and food. The second tack was pursued by Union General William T. Sherman. Calling for "devastation more or less relentless," he laid waste to much of the state of Georgia, entering and burning its capital, Atlanta, on Sept. 1-2, 1864. Marching east to Savannah and the sea, Sherman then hooked north toward Virginia and General Robert E. Lee's army, already besieged from the other direction by Grant's forces.

The Confederacy was doomed: its capital, Richmond, Va., fell on April 3, 1865. Below, Union troops survey the ruins. President Jefferson Davis fled but was captured; at top left, Northern soldiers surround his carriage, en route to Washington. With his troops encircled, starving and bereft of bullets, Lee surrendered to Grant on April 8 at Appomattox Court House, Va., bottom left. Despite some scattered Southern resistance, the Civil War was effectively over. The agrarian South, however valiant its troops in battle, had proved no match for the industrialized North's overwhelming advantage in men, resources and arms.

In His Moment of Triumph, Abraham Lincoln Is Assassinated • 1865

A jubilant crowd gathered outside the White House in the twilight of April 11, three days after Robert E. Lee's surrender, and demanded to hear the Union's victorious President speak. Abraham Lincoln obliged, urging mercy for the vanquished South. It was his last public address. In the crowd was actor and Confederate loyalist John Wilkes Booth, who was plotting to murder the President. Three days later, as Lincoln watched a play at Ford's Theatre, above, Booth fired a single shot into his brain. Lincoln's assassination plunged the North into mourning; his coffin toured the nation on its journey to burial in Illinois. At right, the funeral cortege marches along Fifth Avenue in New York City. The two heads watching the procession from a second-story window at the left of the picture are those of future President Theodore Roosevelt and his brother Elliott.

SURRAT.   BOOTH.   HAROLD.

War Department, Washington, April 20, 1865,

$100,000 REWARD!

THE MURDERER

Of our late beloved President, Abraham Lincoln,

IS STILL AT LARGE.

$50,000 REWARD

Will be paid by this Department for his apprehension, in addition to any reward offered by Municipal Authorities or State Executives.

$25,000 REWARD

Will be paid for the apprehension of JOHN H. SURRATT, one of Booth's Accomplices.

$25,000 REWARD

Will be paid for the apprehension of David C. Harold, another of Booth's accomplices.

EDWIN M. STANTON, Secretary of War.

Swift Justice for Lincoln's Killer and His Allies

Lincoln's assassin, above, was aided in his crime and escape by a cohort of Confederate sympathizers. Booth fled to Virginia and was sheltered by Southern soldiers, but he was fatally shot during his capture on April 26. Four of his fellow plotters were apprehended and tried; they were hanged, left, on July 7, 1865.

"I am tired of fighting ... My people, some of them, have run away to the hills and have no blankets, no food ... Hear me, my chiefs! I am tired; my heart is sick and sad. From where the sun now stands I will fight no more forever." —CHIEF JOSEPH OF THE NEZ PERCÉ, 1877

1865-1900

Into the West

WILD AND MAJESTIC, THE UNTAMED HOME OF NATIVE AMERICANS AND THE BISON, THE VAST SPACES STRETCHING WEST of the Mississippi River to the Pacific Ocean have become *the* frontier in the American imagination, even though colonial Americans thought of the frontier as the Ohio River Valley, and President William Henry Harrison first won fame in the Indian Wars on the Ohio and Indiana frontiers. After the Civil War, the nation's dreams again turned toward the sunset. It took fewer than 30 years for the region to be settled—historian Frederick Jackson Turner declared the frontier era at an end in 1893—yet Americans have spent more than 100 years turning those three decades into myth.

Historical figures helped shape the legends of the West: Lakota chief Sitting Bull, who defeated General George A. Custer at the Battle of the Little Big Horn, later appeared in Buffalo Bill's Wild West show; Wyatt Earp, survivor of the Gunfight at the O.K. Corral, consulted on Hollywood "westerns" in the 1920s; Apache chief Geronimo ended up signing autographs in a booth at the St. Louis World's Fair in 1904. By the time a celebrated photographer of the West, Edward S. Curtis, took this picture in 1901, the Navajo he recorded in Arizona's Canyon de Chelly were no longer the masters of their ancient lands.

The Way West, in Romance and Reality

German-American artist Albert Bierstadt (1830-1902) visited the American West several times in the decades after the Civil War and returned to paint magnificent visions of the region's scenery. Critics of his time accused Bierstadt of overreaching with his canvases, but the outsize scale of such majestic paintings as *Emigrants Crossing the Plains* (1867), which is 67 in. high and 102 in. long, seems appropriate, given the sweeping spaces he portrayed; they became one of the great agents in the mythologizing of the West.

The reality of the pioneers' life, as seen in the picture above of Mormon settlers in 1870, was far less glorious: families faced extremes of weather, new and strange diseases and hostile Indian tribes. The landscapes they traversed—if at times as sublime as a Bierstadt— were often harsh, frequently alien, occasionally deadly and always challenging.

Voyaging Across the Prairies

The long-distance hauler of the West was the Conestoga wagon, a heavy-duty conveyance named for a valley in upstate New York and drawn by mules or oxen. At top right, a train of such wagons carries U.S. Army supplies through the Castle Creek Valley in the Dakota Territory in 1874. Conestoga wagons were used for commercial hauling; settlers traveled in smaller, lighter wagons, later dubbed "prairie schooners."

The 1865 picture at middle right of a pioneer wagon's interior shows it was roomy enough to hold seating and a spinning wheel. At far right, Kansas women dressed up for a picnic cool off in 1878. Settlers like Nebraskan Mary Longfellow built rude homes from bricks of sod, above, and traveled between towns in stagecoaches like the one at right, photographed in 1880.

BETTMANN CORBIS

A Pioneer Boomtown: Buildings of Wood, Visions of Gold

Behold the settlement of Helena, Mont., in 1865, the year after the town was founded when gold was discovered along Last Chance Creek. The main street, Last Chance Gulch, follows the route of the creek up the hillside. Reflecting the nose-thumbing humor of prospectors, the town was called Pumpkinville and Squashtown before residents voted to give it a more serious handle; it was named after St. Helena, Minn., although realists among the settlers dropped the sacred reference from the title. Life in such towns was rude and rough: note the uncollected pile of garbage in front of the grocery at lower left.

Describing a similar boomtown, Carson City, Nev., in *Roughing It*, Mark Twain wrote, "It was a 'wooden' town; its population two thousand souls. The main street consisted of four or five blocks of little white frame stores which were too high to sit down on, but not too high for various other purposes ... They were packed close together, side by side, as if room were scarce in that mighty plain ... The sidewalk was of boards that were more or less loose and inclined to rattle when walked upon." The growth of such boom-towns followed a clear dynamic, as merchants, bankers, grocers, blacksmiths, farriers, pharmacists and prostitutes moved in to serve the miners' needs.

Home, Home on the Range

His great era lasted for little more than three decades—roughly the period between the end of the Civil War and the Yukon Gold Rush—but however brief his shining moment, the cowboy occupies a central place in the American imagination, embodying many of the qualities and themes that are integral to the national experience: the struggle of man against the natural world, the conflicts between European immigrants and Native Americans, the importance of self-reliance and the strenuous life, the power of the gun, the exhilaration of freedom and the promise of the frontier.

"In that land, we led a free and hardy life, with horse and rifle," Theodore Roosevelt wrote in his 1913 autobiography, recalling his days as a North Dakota cattle rancher in the 1880s. "We knew toil and hardship and hunger and thirst; and we saw men die violent deaths as they worked among the horses and cattle, or fought in evil feuds with one another, but we felt the beat of hardy life in our veins, and ours was the glory of work and the joy of living."

The quintessential cowboy experience was the annual roundup of the cattle herd: the steers were then driven from the open range to such railhead towns as Abilene, Texas, or Dodge City, Kans. Below, cowboys "round 'em up" in Wyoming in 1890. Above left, cowpokes play dice at lunchtime in 1880, probably in Colorado.

The symbol of the Great Plains, the bison, was hunted relentlessly; the huge mound of buffalo hides above was photographed as it was being shipped to market from Dodge City in 1874. The U.S. Army joined in the buffalo hunts, deliberately seeking to exterminate the animals that were integral to the lives of the Plains Indians, both as food and as the totemic symbol at the heart of their religion and culture. Almost extinct by 1900, the bison was preserved only by the efforts of far-sighted conservationists.

ROGUES' GALLERY

Although film and fiction have exaggerated the violence of the frontier, shoot-outs, train robberies, hired guns, outlaw gangs, salty saloons and youthful gunmen were the stuff of reality—and thanks to photography, we can look the legends of the West in the eye

Desperadoes

James (Wild Bill) Hickok, above, killed Dave Tutt in 1865 in Springfield, Mo., in a classic frontier showdown. Hickok was killed in a card game in Deadwood, Dakota Territory, in 1876. Confederate sympathizer Jesse James, right, became an outlaw after the Civil War; he was shot dead in 1882. Henry McCarty, a.k.a. "Billy the Kid," below left, was born in New York City; seeking notoriety, he headed west, where he gunned down as many as 21 men before being shot and killed in 1881.

Wyatt Earp, center, became famous for the 1881 Gunfight at the O.K. Corral in Tombstone, Ariz.; he died in Hollywood in 1929, where in his last years he was a consultant on Western life for the movies. At right is Dodge City, Kans., prostitute "Squirrel-Tooth Alice," who sat for a portrait in 1870.

91

93

Elegy for a Way of Life

White settlers moving into the West encountered many different groups of Native American tribes. Southwestern tribes, including the Navajo, Apache and Comanche, were hunters and gatherers but were also agrarian, planting and harvesting crops along waterways in the desert. Tribes of the northern Great Plains, including the Cheyenne and Sioux, were more nomadic, following the buffalo across the grassy prairies and making the bison the totem of their culture. Photographer John C.H. Grabill took the sweeping photo at left of a Lakota Sioux encampment outside Pine Ridge, S.D., in 1891, in the twilight days of the mighty Plains tribe, after the 1890 massacre at Wounded Knee. The image above shows a Lakota tepee and warriors in 1890.

These images record a people in decline, but they also provide a sense of their nomadic lives: the conical tepees, the herd of untethered horses watering in the stream. The Lakota, like their white nemeses, were relative newcomers to this land: they emigrated from the east across the Missouri River to the northern Great Plains after smallpox, a European import, decimated local tribes in the 18th century.

An Indian Victory at the Little Big Horn • 1876

Promoted to the temporary rank of general at age 23 during the Civil War, George Armstrong Custer was a brilliant, courageous U.S. Army commander, but he was also headstrong and hungry for renown. (At left, Custer confers with Native American scouts in the early 1870s, while his Army unit was guarding railroad-building crews.) Knowing he was badly outnumbered as he approached a Sioux and Cheyenne encampment near Montana's Little Big Horn River on June 25, 1876, Custer nonetheless split his Seventh Cavalry command of some 600 men into four separate groups—disregarding orders to await reinforcements—and launched an ill-considered attack against more than 2,500 Indians commanded by Sitting Bull, far right, and Crazy Horse, the fearsome Sioux warrior chiefs.

In the rout that followed, all 264 men under Custer's direct command were slaughtered, along with their vainglorious commander and four others. Recent archaeological digs at the site indicate that Custer's men remained in formation and fought bravely until the last—validating the legend of "Custer's Last Stand" but not excusing the recklessness of his strategy. Below, bodies of the fallen litter the battlefield after the conflict.

Crazy Horse's Shirt

Warrior chief Crazy Horse was known by his fellow Sioux as a "Shirt Wearer," a term denoting his status as a leader in battle. Born around 1840, he was present when Sioux braves killed 29 U.S. soldiers in the Grattan Massacre of 1854. With Sitting Bull, right, he was a leader of the Sioux in the Indian victory at the Little Big Horn 22 years later. His shirt, adorned with human hair, is on display at the National Museum of the American Indian in Washington.

Into the West

A Machine Spans the Wilderness

The "iron horse" was the great tamer of the West, making travel across its wide-open spaces safe, comfortable and swift, even as the locomotive's whistle sounded the death knell for the West's iconic modes of transport: the horse, stagecoach and wagon train. At the close of the Civil War in 1865, there were some 35,000 miles of track in the U.S., reaching as far west as California, but the lines were often isolated and local. Four years later, when the Union Pacific and Central Pacific railroads were connected with a golden spike at Promontory Summit, Utah, the Atlantic and Pacific oceans were stitched together for the first time: Manifest Destiny in parallel lines. By 1890, there were 164,000 miles of track in the U.S.

At right, a Union Pacific train sits on a temporary wooden span over the Green River in Wyoming in 1868 near Citadel Rock, while, at left, masons are building stone piers for a permanent bridge.

Promises of Prosperity

Railroads created their own economic dynamic, as towns and villages sprang up beside the tracks. To create markets for their services, railroad companies promoted the West as a land of opportunity, as in the 1880 Northern Pacific poster above. In order to coordinate railroad timetables, the U.S. was first divided into multiple, coordinated time zones in the 1880s.

98

Massacre at Wounded Knee • 1890

By 1890 the Native Americans of the Great
Plains, outmanned, outgunned and out of
room to retreat, were overwhelmed by white
settlement. Facing the end of their culture,
the Sioux found solace in the Ghost Dance,
a prophetic, wishful vision that the end of
the world was at hand and would be heralded
by the resurrection of slain Indian warriors,
along with the fall of the white man.
Spreading across reservations, the Ghost
Dance alarmed white authorities, who began
arresting influential chiefs.

Sitting Bull, the victor of Little Big Horn,
was shot to death while being taken into
custody on Dec. 15, 1890. While trying to
capture Miniconjou Sioux chief Big Foot on
Dec. 28, 1890, U.S. Army forces massacred
more than 350 men, women and children,
including Big Foot, photographed in death,
above. Right, Sioux survivors of the incident.

99

A Veteran of the Western Wars Comes in from the Cold · 1886

The Apache warrior called himself Goyathlay ("One Who Yawns"), but he became better known by the name the Mexicans gave him, Geronimo. After his wife and children were murdered by settlers in 1850, he became a guerrilla fighter, leading small bands of followers, raiding white settlements and evading U.S. Army cavalrymen (seen at right, in 1885) for decades. Taken into custody several times, he always escaped. Eventually, though, there was nothing left to fight for: the old Apache ways were gone forever.

The longtime outlaw, at center left above, agreed to surrender in 1886; he was placed in a succession of prisons and reservations. Widely admired by Americans of all races for his indomitable spirit, Geronimo spent his last years as an Oklahoma rancher and pop-culture celebrity; he rode in President Theodore Roosevelt's Inaugural parade in 1905.

Oklahoma Land Rush • 1889

In the days leading up to April 22, 1889, some 100,000 land-hungry homesteaders gathered at the border of the 1.9 million-acre area called the Indian Territory. They were preparing to claim vast swaths of real estate—160 free acres for every settler who could grab a plot—previously reserved for the "Five Civilized Tribes": Cherokee, Choctaw, Chickasaw, Creek and Seminole Indians.

At high noon a mounted bugler sounded his horn, and settlers like the gent at left raced into the region later called Oklahoma to stake their claims. By dusk, entire towns had sprung up: a reporter for *Harper's Weekly* noted that "unlike Rome, the city of Guthrie *was* built in a day." Within weeks, Oklahoma City was home to more than 10,000 residents, including "53 physicians, 97 lawyers, 47 barbers, 28 surveyors, 29 real estate agents, and 11 dentists."

The Yukon Gold Rush • 1897

The Oklahoma Land Rush and Yukon Gold Rush are the twin pillars marking the end of America's frontier period. After three men struck gold in Alaska's Klondike region in June 1897, some 100,000 would-be prospectors converged on Seattle by year's end to begin the journey to the gold fields more than 2,500 miles away.

The last half-mile of the gold-seekers' journey was the most difficult passage of the trek: it involved a 1,000-ft. climb up a staircase carved out of solid ice and snow, above, which led to Dead Horse Trail, a path littered with the remains of more than 3,000 pack animals that had frozen to death hauling supplies. Only a third of the treasure hunters who left Seattle managed to reach the gold fields, like the lucky crew at right.

Where History Became Legend: Buffalo Bill's Wild West Show

No period of American life has been so relentlessly mythologized as the settlement of the Western frontier. As early as the 1850s, mountain man and U.S. Army scout Kit Carson was turned into an outsized hero in such "blood and thunder" dime novels as *Kit Carson: The Prince of the Gold Hunters.* Carson's review: "Burn the damn thing."

A key figure in converting the frontier into legend was William F. (Buffalo Bill) Cody (far left, in 1900), an Iowa-born Army scout, bullwhacker, bison hunter, Civil War veteran and superb show-man. Cody toured the world for years with his Wild West show, founded in 1883; audiences in the U.S. and Europe thrilled to such stars as Ohio-born sharpshooter Annie Oakley (left, in 1910) and the show's elaborate set pieces, including stagecoach robberies and shoot-outs. Blurring the line between fantasy and history, Little Big Horn victor Sitting Bull appeared in the show at one time.

At left, the Wild West troupe plays Omaha, Neb., in 1908. Once, when touring in the small town of Marceline, Mo., Cody was driving a buggy as the troupe paraded into town, and he invited a star-struck local boy to join him. "I was mighty impressed," young Walt Disney wrote a relative.

103

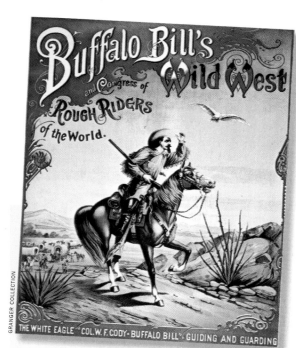

A Really Big Show

The Wild West show featured a spectacular equestrian parade and exhibitions of riding, shooting, wrangling and other cowboy skills. The climax was often an enactment of Custer's Last Stand, with Cody portraying Custer. The poster above is from a Chicago run in 1893.

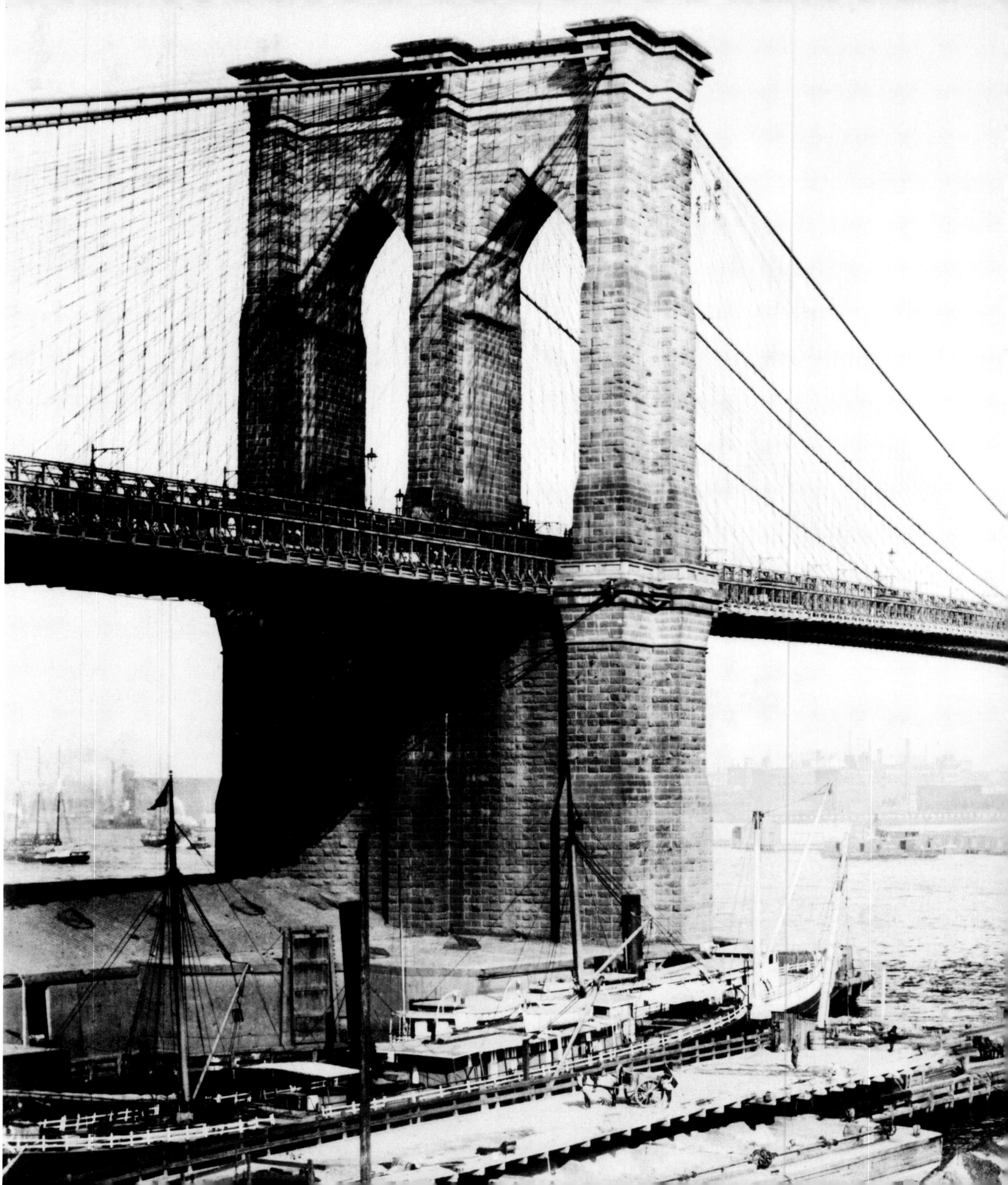

1835-1900

Yankee Ingenuity

WITH TWO REVOLUTIONARY FOUNDING DOCUMENTS, the Declaration of Independence of 1776 and U.S. Constitution of 1787, Americans invented a new kind of society, a grand experiment in personal freedom and representative democracy that would be closely watched and widely imitated around the world. In the mid–19th century, can-do Americans began leading the world in the realm of invention itself, following in the footsteps of the self-taught scientist, inventor and polymath often considered the archetypal American, Benjamin Franklin.

Long regarded as the land of opportunity, America now began to be seen as the frontier of the future, where wonders of science and technology were first imagined, designed and hammered into shape—as a movie camera or a telephone or a new light bulb that changed lives around the planet. This hands-on mastery of nature's laws built a new nation of industrial might, boasting such breathtaking structures as New York's Brooklyn Bridge, left, a creation that must have seemed so futuristic at its dedication in 1883 that it might have appeared to its first admirers to have slipped its moorings in the 20th century and traveled back through time, coming to rest in the age of cowboys and Indians.

"The domain of Science is a republic, and all its citizens are brothers and equals ... barren of man-made gauds and meretricious decorations, upon the one majestic level!"—MARK TWAIN

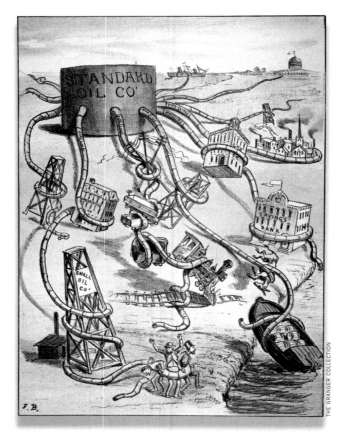

A New Source of Energy: Plentiful, Powerful, Profitable—and Addictive • 1858

At the end of the Civil War, Americans lived by lamplight, their millions of lanterns and lamps lit by kerosene distilled from coal, as whale oil, once plentiful, had become scarce and costly. By the late 1850s, chemists had devised a way to extract kerosene from the foul-smelling petroleum that bubbled out of the ground at a handful of U.S. sites. In 1858 the Seneca Oil Co. asked driller Edwin Drake to see if "crude" oil could be found by drilling into the rock at a creek near Titusville, Pa. (bottom right, above). When the black stuff gushed, it triggered a rush for wealth. Within months, drilling towers replaced trees for miles around Drake's well.

In 1861, 23-year-old Cleveland bookkeeper John D. Rockefeller (top right, above) began refining and distributing oil; 20 years later his Standard Oil Co. dominated the industry, just as the fuel was becoming vital to the nation's rapidly industrializing economy. Using cutthroat pricing, bribery and sabotage, Standard Oil drove its competitors into bankruptcy and dictated the price of oil.

This stranglehold, attacked in the 1884 cartoon above, and later thoroughly exposed by muckraking reporters like Ida Tarbell, finally spurred action. In 1911, the Justice Department used antitrust laws ignored for a generation to break Standard Oil's monopoly into dozens of separate companies.

108

Bell Telephone • 1876

While trying to improve the telegraph, Scots-born American Alexander Graham Bell realized that electricity, when undulating like sound waves, could also reproduce audible sounds, such as speech. In 1876, Bell, then only 29, made the first telephone call, to his assistant: "Mr. Watson, come here. I want to see you."

Months later, Bell showed off the device at the Centennial Exhibition in Philadelphia, touching off a firestorm of enthusiasm. In 1877 Bell helped found the Bell Telephone Co., which began wiring the world—and accelerating life's pace everywhere. At left, the inventor's 1876 sketch of his device; above, some original Bell telephones.

The Kodak Camera.

"You press the button, we do the rest"

(OR YOU CAN DO IT YOURSELF).

The only camera that anybody can use without instructions. Send for the Primer, free.

The Kodak is for sale by all Photo stock dealers.

The Eastman Dry Plate and Film Co.

Price, $25.00 — Loaded for 100 Pictures. Reloading, $2.00. ROCHESTER, N. Y.

Morse Telegraph • 1837

Methods for sending information over wires using electricity had been tested as early as the 1770s, but none were practical. In 1837, Samuel Morse unveiled an electrical key, above, that sent bursts of current over a line in a series of "dots and dashes" that formed a new alphabet, "Morse Code." Allocated $30,000 by Congress to string wires, in 1844 Morse tapped out a biblical passage in Washington, "What hath God wrought?" that was received in a Baltimore train station. A decade later, some 23,000 miles of telegraph wires stitched the nation together.

Eastman Kodak Camera • 1879

Photography was commonplace by the 1870s, but it was complex and costly. Then, in 1879, George Eastman developed a "dry film" that eliminated the need to develop immediately the large glass plates, coated with chemicals, used in the process. Nine years later, Eastman unveiled a new, $25 camera branded "Kodak" (a word Eastman made up): it contained film for 100 photos and was small enough to be sent through the mail to be developed. In 1900, Kodak would unveil the "Brownie," which cost just $1. Eastman's small, handheld cameras liberated photography from professionals and portrait studios and put it in the hands of everyday people. Above, an 1889 Kodak ad; at top, Eastman with one of his cameras in 1890.

INSPIRATION CODIFIED

One of Thomas Edison's most lasting inventions was a new method of invention itself, a unique, formalized process for creating new technologies. The man who famously said that perspiration trumped inspiration created an "invention factory" at his New Jersey headquarters, where tasks were divided among teams of specialists and new gadgets and gizmos were custom-tailored to market demands. This assembly line for innovation resembled the method Edison's friend, Henry Ford, would later pioneer in making autos.

The phonograph he unveiled in 1877, shown in the main picture above, was Edison's favorite invention. Although he suggested the device would be used primarily to record the dying words of famous people, mass audiences turned out to prefer lively music to death rattles. Partially deaf since childhood, Edison continued to redesign and improve

Incandescent Lightbulb

Before Edison, incandescent lights were expensive and short-lived. His key innovation was a new material, a filament of carbonized cotton that lasted for months before burning out, making bulbs both cheap and practical. Above, an 1879 diagram

Motion-Picture Camera

Edison conceived his first motion-picture camera, above, in 1886, but his associate in invention, Briton James W. Dickson, did much of the actual work on the project, dubbed the Kinetescope. Setting the format for such cameras for decades, the device's double row of sprockets pulled flexible film

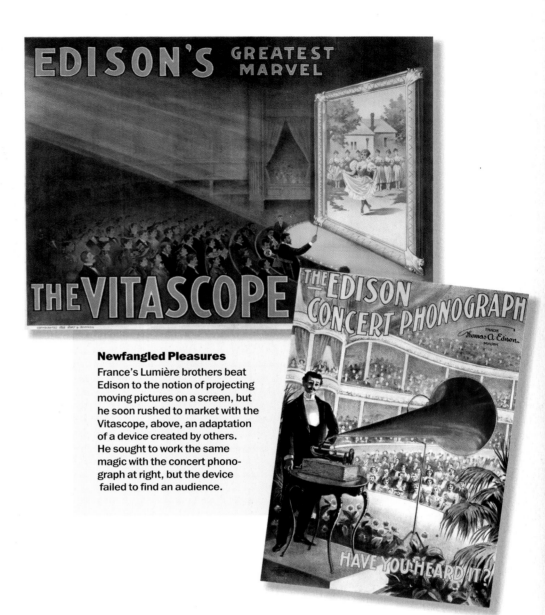

Newfangled Pleasures

France's Lumière brothers beat Edison to the notion of projecting moving pictures on a screen, but he soon rushed to market with the Vitascope, above, an adaptation of a device created by others. He sought to work the same magic with the concert phonograph at right, but the device failed to find an audience.

Motion-Picture Studio

Edison's Kinetescope was a combination motion-picture camera and projector, which filmed movies and showed them to individual viewers through a peephole. These productions were shot in a tarpaper shack in New Jersey, which employees dubbed the "Black Maria" (after the cramped police prisoner wagons of the era, also painted black). The studio rotated on a wheeled track to ensure optimum sunlight inside.

A Modern Prometheus

More than 75 years after his death, Thomas Edison remains a colossus, the down-to-earth tinkerer with less than a year of formal schooling who became a light giver, harnessing electricity to remake the world. Although he did not invent all the technologies he is often given credit for, Edison did perfect the phonograph, the lightbulb and dozens of other devices. Along the way, he was also awarded more than 1,000 U.S. patents.

While he profited handsomely from many of his inventions, Edison was never truly wealthy in the manner of a John D. Rockefeller or an Andrew Carnegie. Instead of owning outright the electric-power, motion-picture or recording industries he made possible, he licensed these technologies to corporations able to market and popularize them in ways he couldn't. Close friend Henry Ford liked to joke that Edison was the world's greatest inventor and worst businessman.

Edison was no saint, and he could be maddeningly stubborn. He remained committed to DC, direct current, whose transmission called for large power plants every few miles, long after the competing AC standard, the alternating current still in use, proved far superior. But this does not diminish his impact: on the day of Edison's funeral in 1931, lights were momentarily dimmed nationwide in his honor.

Expanding Vistas

ONLY 100 YEARS AFTER 13 BRITISH COLONIES UNITED TO WREST THEIR INDEPENDENCE FROM BRITAIN, THE U.S. HAD BECOME AN industrial powerhouse and a beacon of liberty to the world. Around the planet, people dreamed of immigrating to this land of opportunity, where freedom of speech and freedom in the marketplace were reinventing capitalism and Western society. Yet not all was well as the U.S. celebrated its centennial: although great fortunes were being made in America, the nation was increasingly becoming divided between its haves and have-nots, as Congress and the U.S. Supreme Court strongly favored owners over workers, effectively denying the nation's founding promise of equal opportunity for all. Mark Twain denounced the excesses of the "Gilded Age," but even he admired the hustle and bustle of an era of big dreams, as embodied in the lavish buildings of Chicago's "White City," the World's Columbian Exposition of 1893, which drew millions of awed visitors to the Windy City.

BETTMANN CORBIS

"The problem of our age is the proper administration of wealth, so that the ties of brotherhood may still bind together the rich and poor in harmonious relationship."

—ANDREW CARNEGIE, INDUSTRIALIST

ANDREW CARNEGIE

JAY GOULD

J.P. MORGAN

114

In an Age of Gilt Without Guilt, the Rich Get Richer and the Workers Just Get By

Mark Twain dubbed the "raging, tearing, booming" years after the Civil War the Gilded Age, contrasting the Golden Age of ancient Greece with its façade-obsessed modern counterpart. In a time of rapid industrialization, when the U.S. had no income tax and capitalism was unfettered by the U.S. courts or Congress, the industrial titans of the era, popularly known as robber barons, rolled up vast wealth. Titans of steel (Andrew Carnegie), railroads (Jay Gould) and finance (J.P. Morgan, who acted as America's de facto central banker before there was a Federal Reserve) built huge fortunes that still endure, in many cases relying on ruthless business practices later declared illegal.

The temper of the times resembled one historian's pithy summary of the trajectory of imperial Rome: more for fewer. The rich of the Gilded Age surpassed the European monarchs, their role models in wretched excess (on this page, Cornelius Vanderbilt's palatial 1895 "cottage" in Newport, R.I., the Breakers). At the same time, cities teemed with impoverished tenement dwellers, children as young as 7 labored for pitiful wages, and union organizers were murdered by hired thugs. The cynical Gould once bragged, "I can hire one half of the working class to kill the other half."

Not all the barons were robbers: in his essay "Wealth," Carnegie wrote that "the man who dies thus rich dies disgraced." In their later years, Carnegie and other philanthropists gave away the bulk of their fortunes to such causes as education and medical research, improving (and sometimes saving) countless thousands of lives. Gould gave almost nothing to charity.

Manhattan's Corrupt Master

In politics as in commerce, robber-baron tactics proved highly effective. Local party leaders like William (Boss) Tweed, who ran New York City's Democratic machine, Tammany Hall, in the 1860s and early '70s, profited from rampant political corruption, accepting bribes running to millions of dollars for pushing through favorable legislation, deploying police to break strikes and ignoring violations of the law by political allies and donors.

Tweed was eventually brought down by opponents like the incisive political cartoonist Thomas Nast, who stoked public outrage with such images as the 1875 cartoon at right. (Acknowledging Nast's power, Tweed once said, "I don't care so much what the papers say about me. My constituents can't read, but, damn it, they can see pictures!") When Tweed was arrested in 1871, it was Jay Gould who posted his multimillion-dollar bail. But Gould's friendship availed Tweed little: he was convicted and died in jail in 1878.

Liberty Enlightens—and Accommodates–the World

Between the War of 1812 and the start of the Civil War, 5 million immigrants landed on U.S. shores, almost half as many as the total estimated number of Americans in 1815, 7 million. Most of the newcomers arrived from England and Ireland, with the famine-fleeing Irish of the late 1840s and early '50s provoking a backlash: New York City employers seeking laborers used the phrase "No Irish Need Apply" so often that it was shortened to the acronym NINA. In the 25 years after the Civil War, another 10 million immigrants arrived, mostly from northern Europe. Nor had the tide crested: between 1890 and the outbreak of World War I, a third surge of 15 million people landed, primarily from eastern and southern Europe.

New York City and San Francisco were the most frequent ports of entry: on this page, at top, Italian Americans stroll near the Fulton Ferry in Manhattan in 1884; below, youngsters salute the flag in a Manhattan school, circa 1890. At top right, Asian Americans pose in San Francisco's Chinatown, 1890.

America's "open door" immigration policies were part of its growing worldwide appeal, as was its commitment to personal freedoms. The two currents found a perfect embodiment in the Statue of Liberty, dedicated in New York Harbor in 1886, a gift from the nation's old ally in revolution, France. At right, a workman poses with Lady Liberty's copper-clad face early in 1886, before the statue was fully assembled.

Your Message Here?

When funds to complete the statue were scarce in 1885, one wag proposed selling advertising space to fund its construction, a reminder that the nation's obsession with excess commercialism is evergreen.

WINTER MORNING IN THE COUNTRY

AT THE FAIR GROUNDS

BROADWAY, NEW YORK

Currier and Ives: Idealized Portraits Of Life in 19th Century America

Founded by printmaker Nathaniel Currier and businessman James M. Ives, the publishing house Currier and Ives enjoyed enormous popularity in the 19th century; its color lithographs served as visual journalism, at a time when newspaper presses were unable to reproduce photos and paintings. Currier's early works often portrayed newsmaking disasters: big-city fires, train wrecks and steamboat explosions.

The firm's hand-colored lithographs include political cartoons and maps, but America's favorites, then and now, are the portrayals of everyday life painted by the firm's numerous artists. Much like painter Norman Rockwell's work in the 20th century, these soothing images hold up an idealizing mirror to American life, while also capturing the land's regional diversity and recording in journalistic detail the styles, labors and customs of the times.

THE RIVER SIDE

One Hell of a Hard Sell

Look closely, and you'll see the face of the devil forming in the smoke above a burning Chicago in this 1890 advertisement. An estimated 200 to 300 people died in the 1871 conflagration, while some 90,000 people were left homeless, almost 1 of every 3 residents. The fire claimed 17,500 buildings, while some $220 million in property value went up in smoke. Small wonder the quickly rebuilt city was resplendent with brick and iron.

The Great Chicago Fire • 1871

By the mid–19th century, the transportation hub of Chicago had become the Midwest's colossus of trade. Railroad and Great Lakes shipping lines converged on the dynamic city on the west shore of Lake Michigan, the funnel through which beef from Montana, iron ore from northern Minnesota, grain from Nebraska and hundreds of other commodities passed each day. Yet if the goods it handled traveled in metal ships and on steel rails, Chicago was still primarily a city made of wood. On Oct. 8, 1871, when drought and wind conditions seemed to conspire to transform a small local fire into a raging, uncontrollable inferno, the Illinois port experienced the most extensive disaster yet to strike a major American city.

A charming fable maintains that the fire was caused when a cow owned by Patrick and Catherine O'Leary kicked over a lantern; a newspaperman later confessed he concocted the tale. But the fire did break out near their home on the city's west side, then jumped the Illinois River. When it burned itself out two days later, almost 4 sq. mi. of the city's core had been leveled, above. Yet gutsy Chicagoans rebuilt quickly, and only 22 years later their restored city played host to the World's Columbian Exposition, a landmark in U.S. history.

The Johnstown Flood • 1889

In the annals of great U.S. calamities, western Pennsylvania's Johnstown Flood stands out for the swiftness with which it claimed more than 2,200 lives. The flood's effects were magnified by Johnstown's geography: its buildings perched on the sides of steep hills near the confluence of the Little Conemaugh River and the smaller Stony Creek. On May 28, when waters from the heaviest rains ever recorded in the region breached the South Fork Dam, located some 14 miles upstream and 450 ft. above the town, floodwaters roared into the Johnstown Valley at an estimated 40 m.ph., surging to heights over 60 ft. As the raging waters swept in, bearing trees and debris, there was nowhere for the town's 30,000 citizens to run.

The dam, owned by a sporting club catering to the wealthy, had been weakened by alterations, contributing to the disaster. The president of the American Red Cross, Clara Barton, rushed to the scene and helped lead relief efforts, establishing a lasting reputation for her fledgling organization. Below, a resident poses on a tree driven through a home by floodwaters.

121

Mark Twain's America

Much as Benjamin Franklin appears to embody all the varied interests of early Americans, Mark Twain seems to have earned his spurs on every frontier of 19th century America. Born Samuel Clemens in 1835, he grew up in the small town of Hannibal, Mo. Fulfilling a boyhood dream, he became a steamboat pilot on the Mississippi River, then served a short tour of duty in the Civil War; later he joined the great silver rush in Carson City, Nev., meeting desperadoes and "varmints" and absorbing the West's tall tales and yarns. Twain chronicled his life and times in such popular journalistic accounts as *Roughing It* and *Life on the Mississippi*, in a voice that caught America's energy, informality and rawboned good humor.

In his powerful, challenging 1884 novel, *The Adventures of Huckleberry Finn*, Twain probed the plight of an unlikely pair of runaways, an adolescent white boy and a black slave, in the years before the Civil War. Until his death in 1910, Twain was America's chief gadfly, agnostic and debunker of pomposity. Here he poses for a portrait in 1890 in Connecticut; at top, the original cover of *Huckleberry Finn* and Twain's handwritten manuscript of the novel's first chapter.

Anarchy in the U.S. • 1886

The increasing economic polarization of the U.S. in the late 19th century divided national sentiment, as owners and managers battled union leaders and workers in a series of highly publicized strikes, even as homegrown anarchists inspired by current European political trends called for outright revolution in the streets.

The low-grade labor wars erupted in public violence in Chicago's Haymarket Riot on May 4, 1886. Three days before, some 80,000 labor unionists had gone on strike, calling for an 8-hr. workday and marching down Michigan Avenue in one of the world's first May Day observances. On the 4th, workers were rallying near Haymarket Square when a bomb was set off, killing eight officers; policemen then opened fire, killing a number of civilians. Eight anarchists were tried and found guilty of murder; four were hanged in 1887.

FOR BLACKS: STAGNATION, SEGREGATION, JIM CROW AND "SEPARATE BUT EQUAL"

The North's victory in the Civil War proved hollow for African Americans, who found themselves consigned to virtual slavery in the South's sharecropping system and relegated to inferior status in a nation that legalized segregation

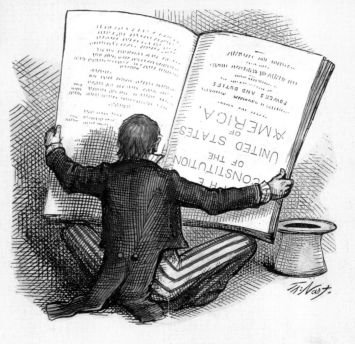

123

Segregation by Jim Crow–and the U.S. Supreme Court

Blacks were welcome on America's burgeoning railroads in the late 19th century—as long as they were working as porters, like the man above, or riding in segregated, second-class carriages. After the Civil War, new rights for blacks were written into the Constitution in Amendments 13, 14 and 15. But Reconstruction in the South, which Abraham Lincoln had intended to be a period of healing, exacerbated sectional hatreds and led to the founding of the Ku Klux Klan in the 1860s; the guerrilla, racist organization was devoted to keeping blacks out of mainstream society. When the election of 1876 ended in a virtual Electoral College tie, as shown in the cartoon at right, a deal was cut: Ohio's Rutherford B. Hayes became President in return for his pledge to withdraw Northern troops from the South, effectively ending Reconstruction.

Across the nation, segregation was enforced by Jim Crow laws, until, in 1896, the U.S. Supreme Court approved the division of the races in the case of *Plessy v. Ferguson,* ruling that blacks deserved only "separate but equal" status in the nation's railways, schools and other public places. It was a prescription for second-class citizenship. One bright spot for blacks seeking advancement was Alabama's Tuskegee Institute, top right, led by legendary black educator Booker T. Washington.

Conserving America's Natural Heritage

For long decades in American history, the natural bounty of the land was so abundant as to seem inexhaustible. But warning signs emerged in the late 1800s: the mighty herds of bison that once roamed the range had been hunted almost to extinction, the huge, sun-blocking flocks of passenger pigeons seen no more. Audubon's American Eden had become an industrial colossus, its cities smoky and fouled with waste. As early as 1864, President Abraham Lincoln signed an Act of Congress ceding the Yosemite Valley, below, to the state of California, to be held in perpetuity as a natural preserve; in 1872 Congress established the Yellowstone region in Wyoming as the first U.S. National Park.

Scottish-American naturalist John Muir, left circa 1902, helped save the Yosemite Valley from development and convinced Americans of the necessity of conservation.

America Declares Its Independence—in Sport

Befitting citizens of a nation founded in rebellion, Americans prefer to invent their own sports. Baseball derives loosely from bat-and-ball games played in Britain since the mid-1700s; Civil War Union soldiers played the game in two forms. By 1886, professional teams like the Boston Braves and New York Giants, above center, were drawing huge crowds.

Basketball was created in Massachusetts in 1891 by Canadian-born Dr. James A. Naismith, who was seeking a fast indoor game for winter play; at left, he holds the first hoop, a peach basket. George Ferris' 264-ft.-high eponymous joyride wheel made its debut at Chicago's 1893 World's Columbian Exposition and swept the planet into its metallic embrace.

125

Enduring Classics of Everyday Life

The mail-order catalog was a revolution in retailing; it cut America's vast expanses down to size, bringing urban products to small towns across the land. Sears, Roebuck & Co., dreamed up by a railroad station agent and a watchmaker in 1887, grew so quickly that by 1894 its catalog had expanded to 322 pages.

P. T. Barnum was America's greatest showman, a panjandrum of ballyhoo whose hoaxes and freak shows amused the "suckers" he insisted were born every minute. Operating under a variety of names and incarnations, the circus he founded in 1871 became a long-lived, beloved sideshow on the American scene.

Physician and pharmacist John Stith Pemberton invented Coca-Cola in the late 1880s, combining coca leaves, kola nuts and other ingredients that remain a closely guarded secret. Although cocaine was removed from the formula in 1904, the popular carbonated beverage has become a global emblem of American culture. In a 1950 cover story, TIME said, "It is simpler, harder evidence than the Marshall Plan or a Voice of America broadcast that the U.S. has gone out into the world to stay." Above right, an advertising poster for "Coke" from the 1880s.

Imperial Dreams

BEHOLD THEODORE ROOSEVELT AND HIS ROUGH RIDERS, POSING ATOP CUBA'S SAN JUAN HILL AFTER their gutsy charge swept Spanish soldiers from its heights on July 1, 1898. However grand the sight, it might have astonished the Founding Fathers of the U.S., who rejoiced in their new nation's geographic isolation, which kept Americans an ocean's width from international conflicts. Yet in the 1890s heyday of the pulse-quickening marches of John Philip Sousa, some Americans began to entertain imperial dreams—including the ever martial Roosevelt, then Assistant Secretary of the U.S. Navy. The "jingos" seized upon ongoing unrest in Cuba, just off the tip of Florida, where rebels were fighting their Spanish masters, whose ancient colonial empire was in decline. Aided by a hawkish press, the U.S. quickly declared and won what Roosevelt called a "splendid little war" with Spain. America, born of revolution against an empire, was now itself an imperial power, with all the consequences, intended and unintended, such power conferred.

"I should welcome almost any war, for I think this country needs one." —THEODORE ROOSEVELT, PRIVATE LETTER, 1897

Remembering the *Maine,* the U.S. Takes Over an Empire • 1898

America rolled into the 1890s with a swagger in its step. Despite the Panic of 1893, which threw the economy off-kilter for several years, it was an age of robust progress and big dreams. As the nation's frontier era was ending, some Americans began to cast longing glances at new frontiers for expansion. In the Pacific, Hawaii and Spain's colony in the Philippines beckoned. Much closer to home, in Cuba, rebellious natives were waging a guerrilla war against Spain. When the Spanish responded with inhumane clampdowns, U.S. expansionists, or "jingos," condemned the tactics and urged Spain to leave the island.

As tensions rose, the battleship U.S.S. *Maine,* left, blew up in the harbor of Cuba's capital, Havana, on Feb. 15, 1898. The cause of the blast is still not known, but the tragedy sparked a national outcry for war. In a conflict that lasted only 113 days, a U.S. fleet under Commodore George Dewey whipped a Spanish fleet in Manila Bay, and a U.S. expeditionary force landed in Cuba, took control of Guantánamo Bay, top, and defeated Spain's troops in battles at El Caney and San Juan Hill, where the Spanish soldiers at right were wounded.

At the end of the Spanish-American War, the U.S. inherited an empire: Spain ceded Cuba, the Philippines, Puerto Rico and the Pacific island of Guam to the U.S. In 1903 President Theodore Roosevelt awarded independence to Cuba but retained U.S. control of Guantánamo Bay.

Bogged Down in the Philippines • 1898-1913

In Spain's largest colony, the Philippine Islands in the South Pacific, residents hated Spanish rule as much as did the Cubans in the Americas. In the 1890s rebels began staging guerrilla raids against the Spanish. The fighting escalated into a full-fledged rebellion in 1896, and a peace pact reached in December 1897 scarcely had time to take hold before the U.S. declared war on Spain in the spring of 1898.

The U.S. struck quickly in the Philippines. On May 1, 1898, only a week after war was declared, Commodore George Dewey's U.S. squadron routed Spain's puny fleet of 12 outmoded vessels in Manila Bay. By the end of July, some 11,000 U.S. troops had landed near Manila, where they faced a Spanish army holding the capital city. At right, U.S. soldiers dig into positions outside Manila. Neither Spain nor the U.S. wanted the sizable army of native insurgents on the scene to take control of the islands: after a series of brief skirmishes, the last of which was staged for show, the Spanish formally surrendered to the U.S. on Aug. 14. Above, a regiment of Nebraska Volunteers departs Manila in 1899.

The rebels believed they had only exchanged one colonial power for another; in the Philippine Insurrection that soon followed, Filipinos battled more than 120,000 occupying U.S. troops until 1902, when peace was reached—although some rebels fought until 1913—15 years after the fighting began.

An Island Paradise Joins Hands with the Mainland • 1898

Brought together for the first time in 1810 under a single king, Kamehameha I, Hawaii endured for less than a century as an independent, unified nation. The chain of islands came of age just as America's eyes turned toward the Pacific. By mid-century, Hawaii was the leading port of call for New England whalers and merchant ships headed for the Far East, and the cultivation of fruit and sugar began to dominate the islands' economy. An 1875 treaty asserting that Hawaiians would sell these products only to the U.S. made the young nation financially reliant on America; an 1888 agreement ceding Pearl Harbor to the U.S. sealed its military dependence.

When Queen Liliuokalani, left, set out to curb U.S. influence in 1893, the senior U.S. diplomat on the scene called in Marines from a nearby gunboat, who deposed the Queen and set up a new government. The "Republic of Hawaii" was dominated by Americans: its president was missionary Sanford Dole, who petitioned Washington for annexation. Five years later, the republic ceased to exist and Hawaii officially became a U.S. territory (below, the formal ceremony is held in 1898). Statehood, welcomed by the vast majority of Hawaiians, followed in 1959.

The Reluctant Expansionist

"You may be sure," William McKinley told a friend shortly before becoming President in 1897, "that there will be no jingo nonsense under my Administration." The prediction was sincere but mistaken: America embarked on a major period of expansion under a man who was the most hesitant of imperialists. During McKinley's four years in office, Hawaii was annexed, Cuba and the Philippines invaded and Puerto Rico and Guam acquired, while planning for the Panama Canal was initiated.

McKinley was an unassuming man, more interested in finance and taxes than colonies or conquest. Calling himself "the advance agent of prosperity," McKinley ran in 1896 on a platform of support for banking and industry, increased foreign trade and protective tariffs. Most of these issues were quickly forgotten after he took office and the imperial imperative took on a life of its own. When he ran for re-election in 1900, McKinley's slogan had become "Prosperity at Home, Prestige Abroad," and he spoke of little other than foreign policy.

McKinley did not live to realize his platform: on Sept. 6, 1901, he was shot by anarchist Leon Czolgosz while visiting the Pan-American Exposition in Buffalo, N.Y.; at left, his funeral procession parades through Washington. Vice President Theodore Roosevelt, the most ardent of expansionists, succeeded him.

133

An Uncommon Voice for the Common Man

William Jennings Bryan may be the most influential U.S. politician never to occupy the White House, although it wasn't for lack of trying. In between waging three presidential campaigns, he won several major battles (for women's suffrage and Prohibition), lost others (such as a plan to convert the U.S. monetary system to a silver standard) and raised his voice in arguments that preoccupy the Republic to this day (such as the debate between evolution and creationism). Bryan was also a leader of the isolationists who opposed the aggressive international agenda of the Republicans of his day, but he was in the minority in this view.

The populist Democrat was an electrifying orator who enthralled his party's 1896 convention with a speech supporting a silver standard. "You shall not press down upon the brow of labor this crown of thorns, you shall not crucify mankind upon a cross of gold," he roared, to rapturous applause. "The Great Commoner," shown campaigning at right, lost to William McKinley that year, again in 1900 and to William Howard Taft in 1908. Bryan later served as Secretary of State under President Woodrow Wilson but resigned in protest over policies he felt were bringing America closer to involvement in World War I. His last public act was to serve as counsel for the prosecution in the 1925 Scopes "monkey trial."

Full Speed Ahead

AMERICA SAILED INTO THE 20TH CENTURY WITH ALL FLAGS FLYING. GALVANIZED by victory in the Spanish-American War, driven by new visions of empire and energized by a steady influx of immigrants seeking opportunity, Americans sensed their horizons were still expanding—and proved it by trading in their horses and buggies for motorcars. Commanding the ship of state was a human dynamo, President Theodore Roosevelt, the most active and effective Chief Executive in decades. In an age of transforming new energies, T.R. seemed to encompass and embody all the strands of American life: he was equally at home in the parlors of New York City socialites and in the raucous saloons of North Dakota frontiersmen.

Advocating "the strenuous life," Roosevelt battled trusts, cartels and the "malefactors of great wealth," protected the nation's open spaces by creating new national parks, assembled the Great White Fleet for the U.S. Navy (seen here in 1907), sent it on a round-the-world cruise to promote U.S. might and bullied Central Americans in order to cut a canal across the Panama isthmus. The 20th century, which TIME co-founder Henry Luce would later call "The American Century," was off and running, full speed ahead.

"Far better it is to dare mighty things, to win glorious triumphs even though checkered by failure, than to rank with those poor spirits who neither enjoy nor suffer much because they live in the gray twilight that knows neither victory nor defeat." —THEODORE ROOSEVELT

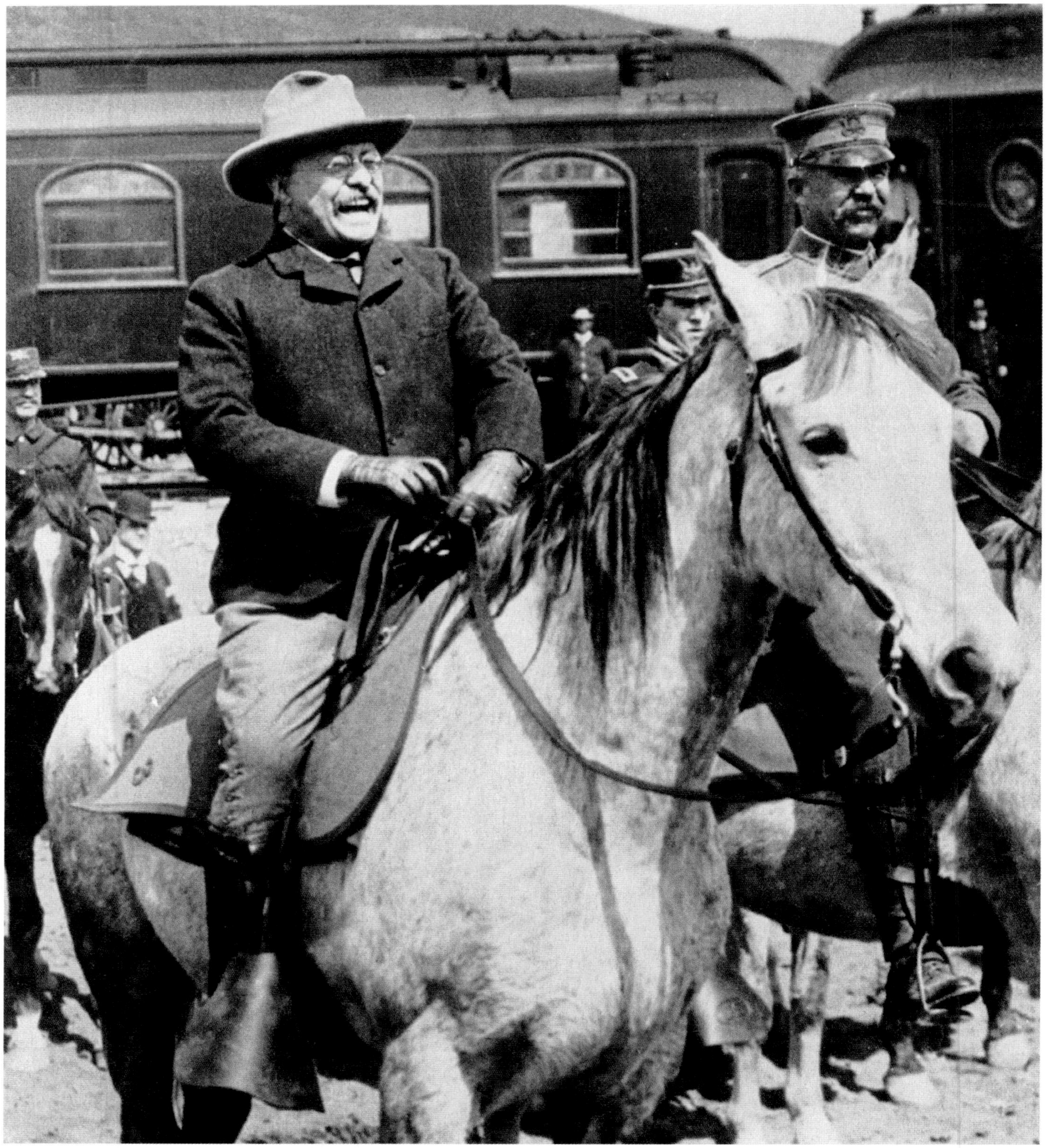

Saddle Up!

"That damned cowboy is President!" thundered G.O.P. boss Mark Hanna after Theodore Roosevelt succeeded William McKinley, victim of an assassin's bullet, in 1901. Roosevelt's popularity after his charge up San Juan Hill in the Spanish-American War had carried him into the vice presidency; now he galloped into the presidency, transforming the institution with his compulsive energy and wide-ranging interests. Soon Roosevelt was using the "bully pulpit" of the White House (he was the first to call the Executive Mansion by that name and built the mansion's West Wing) to drive the nation's agenda. Americans marveled as T.R. brokered peace between mine owners and labor unions, busted trusts, battled the railroads, founded powerful new federal agencies and created vast new national parks.

LEFT: UNDERWOOD & UNDERWOOD; RIGHT: NATIONAL ARCHIVES

A Man, a Plan, a Canal

Defying critics who accused him of "jingoism," Roosevelt never doubted that the U.S. was the natural leader of the Americas. He helped engineer a 1903 revolution in Colombia that led to the formation of a new nation, Panama—across which Americans soon began to build a canal, below. Completed in 1914, the Panama Canal cut in half the time and distance required for ships to move between the Atlantic and Pacific oceans. In 1977, after Panamanian protests, President Jimmy Carter and Congress agreed to allow Panama to take control of the Canal Zone; the formal transfer of sovereignty took place in 1999.

138

The Jungle • 1906

In an age of muckrakers and growing appeals for government regulation of industrial practices, Upton Sinclair's novel exposed unsanitary conditions at the Chicago Union Stockyards, above, and sparked the passage of the federal Pure Food and Drug Act.

A Skyscraper Tragedy • 1911

On March 25, 146 female garment workers were killed when a raging fire devastated the top floors of a building in New York City's Greenwich Village; many of the victims leaped to their death from ninth-story windows, above. The fire dramatized the severe limitations of the laissez-faire capitalism widely practiced in the era, which allowed owners to exploit workers with a minimum of outside regulation: the seamstresses of the Triangle Shirtwaist Co. were paid $1.50 for their 72-hr. workweek. The tragedy led to new laws regulating workers' compensation and building safety.

Tenement Life

An immigrant family does piecework for the garment trade in a crowded New York City tenement, left. The increasing tide of immigrants arriving from southern Europe in the first years of the new century would spark a backlash in the 1920s and the passage of laws establishing quotas for immigration according to national origin.

139

Long March to the Voting Booth

American women's journey to equality with men began at the 1848 Seneca Falls, N.Y., convention led by Elizabeth Cady Stanton and Lucretia Mott. But their movement lost traction in the era of Civil War and Reconstruction, and it wasn't until the late 1800s that U.S. women again began demanding expanded rights, including the franchise. "Suffrage is the pivotal right, the one that underlies all other rights," declared Susan B. Anthony, the outspoken 19th century women's leader. The suffragists were often met with scorn and condescension from their husbands and employers, but as more and more women left their families to live and work in cities or to attend college, the pressure for reform mounted.

Gaining fresh impetus from the example of British suffragists, 15,000 women marched down Fifth Avenue in New York City in May 1912, above, to call for the vote. Their movement was temporarily side-tracked by World War I, but in 1918 President Woodrow Wilson became a prominent advocate of their cause, and on Aug. 18, 1920, the 19th Amendment to the Constitution was ratified, guaranteeing women the vote.

Program, Suffrage March on Washington • 1913
Fifty years before the Rev. Martin Luther King Jr. led blacks on a march for civil rights in Washington, American women rallied in the capital to demand the vote; this program enlists Joan of Arc in the suffragist cause.

Unions Lead the Battle for Improved Working Conditions

Before America was born, it had labor pains. The first recorded strike in U.S. history took place in 1768, when New York City tailors stopped working to protest a cut in wages. Early American unions resembled European guilds, and a distinctly American brand of trade unionism emerged only in the late 19th century, in step with the Industrial Revolution. At a time when 12-hr. workdays were the norm, wages were lean, and many workplaces were filthy and dangerous, the movement fought for shorter hours, fair wages and safe working conditions—and slowly, painfully, grudgingly, progress was made.

Extremists flourished on both sides of the union-management divide. At this July 1914 Industrial Workers of the World rally in New York City's Union Square, anarchist leader Alexander Berkman, who had shot and stabbed industrialist Henry Clay Frick in 1892 and served 14 years in prison for the attempted murder, speaks just one week after a failed attempt to bomb the home of oil magnate John D. Rockefeller, which he may have taken part in. Most Americans rejected such extreme tactics, however, and union membership stalled at just 10% of the work force before World War I. In the Great Depression, the labor movement adopted a "pure and simple" approach, stressing better wages and benefits, and membership soared. By the end of World War II, more than 12 million Americans belonged to a union.

AMERICA'S SHAME: CHILD LABOR

In 1900, census officials estimated that 1.75 million children ages 10 to 15 were employed full time in America; the real number was probably higher. In another sign of the prevalence of child labor, one in four workers in Southern cotton mills in 1900 was under 15

Chronicler of Childhood Misery

Although America's spirit was expansive in the early 1900s, the nation was riven by social inequities. Photographer Lewis W. Hine was one of those who sought to capture injustice on camera, traveling across the country to document the scourge of child labor, sometimes posing as a Bible salesman to gain entry to factories and plants. Hine's images on this page show children toiling as coal miners in Pennsylvania, cotton pickers in Texas and weavers in South Carolina. Luther Watson, 14, above, lost his arm in an industrial accident.

Heeding calls for reform, Congress passed legislation in 1916 and 1918 that restricted child labor, but the Supreme Court struck down the laws as violating freedom of trade.

Calamity at the Golden Gate • 1906

In one of the greatest natural disasters in U.S. history, California's storied boomtown, San Francisco, was devastated on April 18, 1906, by an early-morning earthquake. The cataclysmic event leveled hundreds of buildings and sparked raging fires that consumed vast tracts of the hilly city, still largely built of wood.

Although an estimated 80% of the "Gateway to the Pacific" was destroyed, leaving as many as 300,000 people homeless, city authorities deliberately undercounted the number of dead, claiming only 567 people had perished. The correct number is now estimated to be closer to 3,000. U.S. Army troops stepped in to keep order in the stricken town. The quake helped shift California's center of gravity from San Francisco to Los Angeles and jump-started the fledgling science of seismology.

BETTMANN CORBIS

145

A Nation on the Move

As if on schedule, the new century brought innovations in transportation that quickly began to transform American life. Henry Ford and a host of other inventive automakers made Detroit and the upper Midwest a dynamic new center of industrial creativity, while Ford put technology in gear with democracy by producing a motorcar cheap enough to be purchased by the workers who made it. Yet even as cars began replacing horse-drawn carriages on the nation's roads, another revolution was, well, in the air.

The airplane and the automobile grew up in tandem: Orville and Wilbur Wright, Ohio bicycle mechanics, got their *Flyer* airborne five years before Ford unveiled his revolutionary Model T. In this picture, Wilbur Wright is making an airborne circumnavigation of Manhattan Island in 1909. The new motor-driven vehicles abolished old constraints of time and distance: soon suburbs would begin sprouting around America's cities, while the nostrils of city dwellers, long acclimated to horse manure, entertained a bracing aroma that smelled of the future: gasoline fumes.

UNDERWOOD & UNDERWOOD—CORBIS

AP IMAGES

Main Street's Heyday of the Five-and-Dime

Retailer F.W. Woolworth reinvented the way Americans bought goods, bringing an industrial-age approach to sales when he opened his first store in 1879. Unlike the familiar general store, Woolworth's stores eschewed haggling; all goods were priced at 5¢ or 10¢ and laid out for customers to handle, rather than kept behind a counter. As Woolworth's five-and-dimes proliferated, he used his buying power to leverage lower prices for his customers, a policy followed decades later by Sam Walton's Wal-Mart stores.

With 596 stores generating $53 million in sales by 1912, Woolworth's became one of America's first national brand names. In 1913 Woolworth built the world's tallest skyscraper, the "cathedral of commerce" in Manhattan, right—and paid for its construction in cash.

146

Landmark Products

George Eastman's $1 camera (1900) made photography a national fad. King Gillette's revolutionary blades (1903) were one of the first products designed to be thrown away.

LEFT, TOP: HENRY GROSKINSKY—TIME LIFE PICTURES; BOTTOM: SCIENCE MUSEUM—SCIENCE AND SOCIETY PICTURE LIBRARY

EDWIN LEVICK—HULTON ARCHIVE—GETTY IMAGES

Henry Ford's Three Revolutions • 1913

Henry Ford, proudly perched on a prototype Model T at right in 1907, spearheaded three American revolutions. Unveiling the Model T in 1908, he made the automobile affordable to the masses for the first time. Five years later, in 1913, Ford and his engineers perfected the moving assembly line, above. With stationary workers building autos traveling past them on chain-driven lines, Ford increased his rate of production and cut prices on his cars; the Model T advertised for $850 in 1909, right, cost $290 in 1924.

Ford's third great revolution was social: in 1914, he began offering his workers the unheard-of sum of $5 for a day's work; labor prices around the nation rose in response, and poor Southern blacks moved north in large numbers to find work.

1914-19

Mission In Europe

AS HE LEFT THE PRESIDENCY, GEORGE WASHINGTON famously warned his countrymen against the "insidious wiles of foreign influence." For 100 years Americans heeded those words, secure in their isolation from Europe. That period ended when the U.S. inherited Spain's crumbling colonial empire in the wake of the Spanish-American War of the late 1890s. After Europe's great powers cascaded into war in August 1914, the U.S. refused to take sides in the conflict; tens of millions of Americans traced their heritage to one or another of the nations at war, leaving the U.S. deeply divided over which side to support. Yet though President Woodrow Wilson's stated policy was one of neutrality, by 1916 U.S. trade with Germany had been reduced 99% while trade with Britain and France had tripled.

In February 1917, Germany began waging submarine warfare against all merchant shipping in the Atlantic; months later, the revelation of the "Zimmerman Telegram," which detailed a German plot to start a war between Mexico and the U.S., put Americans firmly on the side of Britain and France. In March of 1918, the first U.S. troops began arriving "Over There." In this picture, U.S. soldiers are firing 37-mm machine guns at German troops in the Argonne Forest in the fall of 1918, scene of the heaviest U.S. engagement in the conflict.

149

**"Johnnie show the Hun
Who's a son of a gun
Hoist the flag and let her fly
Yankee Doodle do or die."**

—GEORGE M. COHAN, *OVER THERE*

In the War's Wake, Americans Debate Isolationism and Internationalism

America's military triumph in the Great War was followed by a diplomatic muddle that dashed the utopian expectations raised by victory. Although U.S. President Woodrow Wilson was given a triumphal welcome to the 1919 Paris Peace Conference (at left, his motorcade is shown passing Maxim's restaurant), the idealistic former president of Princeton University was unable to persuade the U.S. Senate and the American people to abandon America's cherished isolationist stance on the world stage and join the new international body he envisioned as a global peacekeeper, the League of Nations. Wilson suffered a debilitating stroke on Oct. 2, 1919, during a speaking tour in support of the league, and his wife and Cabinet ran his Administration during its last 17 months.

The Paris Peace Conference produced the Treaty of Versailles, which imposed crippling, punitive terms on Germany. Twenty years later, an embittered, defiant Germany would lead Europe, and then the U.S., into another major conflict, World War II.

A War in Europe Transforms America

After the U.S. Congress declared war on Europe's Central Powers in April 1917, it took almost a year for American forces to mobilize and ship out in significant numbers, but tens of thousands of fresh troops and a bottomless reservoir of supplies began to reach the trenches of France and Belgium in early 1918. At St. Mihiel in September of that year, the first battle in which Americans fought on their own, more than 1 million U.S. troops cut off a German salient and ended the Central Powers' hopes for a battlefield victory. Germany signed the Armistice two months later.

151

At left, American "doughboys" are shown hauling ammunition at St. Baussant, during the St. Mihiel campaign; in these first decades of the 20th century, warfare was still a matter of mules, mud, mildew and misery.

The War to End All Wars brought carnage on a scale previously unknown in human conflict. Trench warfare and the first large-scale uses of air power, machine guns and poison gas (U.S. troops in gas masks are seen above, in the Lorraine region of France), combined to kill more than 10 million fighting men. The war claimed another 20 million lives through disease, hunger and other indirect causes.

Entering late, the U.S. bore relatively little of this cost: some 112,000 Americans perished in the fighting, while an entire generation of Europe's young men was slaughtered. But America's experience in the Great War, as it was then called, transformed the nation in others ways. Having financed and fed the Allies, and having helped break the battlefield stalemate, the U.S. emerged from the war as a major global power—like it or not. As a U.S. officer declared on July 4, 1917, at the tomb of a French aristocrat who had helped America's rebel colonists win their freedom 134 years before: "Lafayette, we are here!"

Shoving Off • 1917-18

Above, troops of the American Expeditionary Force depart for Europe in 1917. The U.S. declared war on Germany on April 6 of that year, and on Austria-Hungary eight months later, but America never formally joined the Allied Powers, led by France and Britain; instead, the U.S. went to war as an "Associated Power."

At left, new soldier T.P. Laughlin says a fond farewell to his family in 1917. By the war's end, 19 months after the U.S. entered the conflict, some 4 million Americans were in uniform; an estimated 2 million had served overseas, and three-quarters of that number had seen combat.

American troops played their strongest role in the Meuse-Argonne Offensive that was launched in France in late September 1918, a pivotal year in which the Central Powers mounted a strong spring offensive but were ultimately beaten back by the Western Allies, leading to the Armistice declared on Nov. 11, 1918.

A Nation at War • 1917-18

Americans rallied to support their men (and a small number of women) in uniform during the conflict they called the Great War (the term World War I was introduced after the century's second great global struggle began in 1939). But rationing of food and gas wasn't mandatory during the war years, and the relatively brief war effort did not affect life on the home front as powerfully as World War II would.

These scenes capture Americans' everyday lives during the war years. Clockwise from top left, black soldiers gather at a segregated club in Newark, N.J.; farmers parade in New York City; immigrant women play Betsy Ross; and Charlie Chaplin stands on the shoulders of Douglas Fairbanks at a war-bond rally on Wall Street in New York City.

Graphic Patriotism

America's participation in the war was brief; its fleeting impact on pop culture is best captured in recruiting posters and a famous battle-cry of a song.

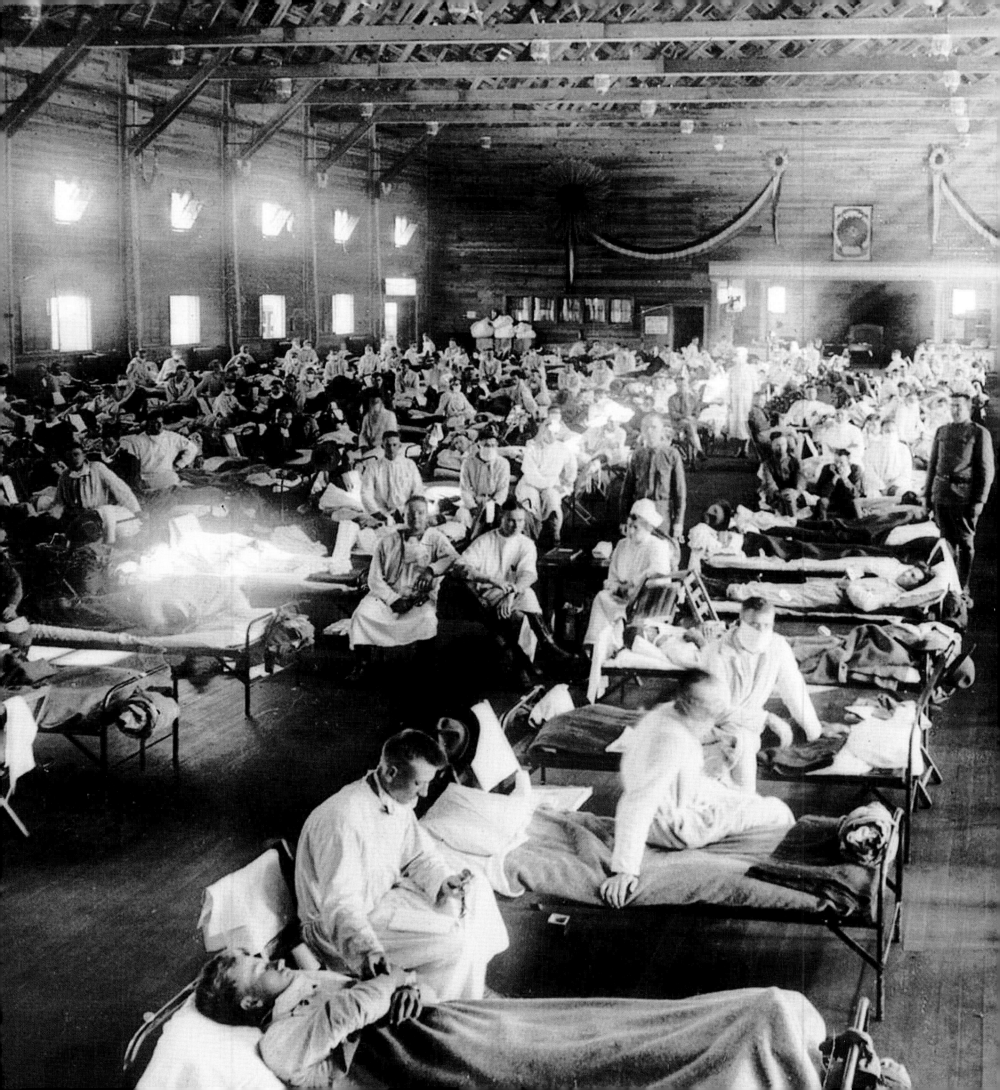

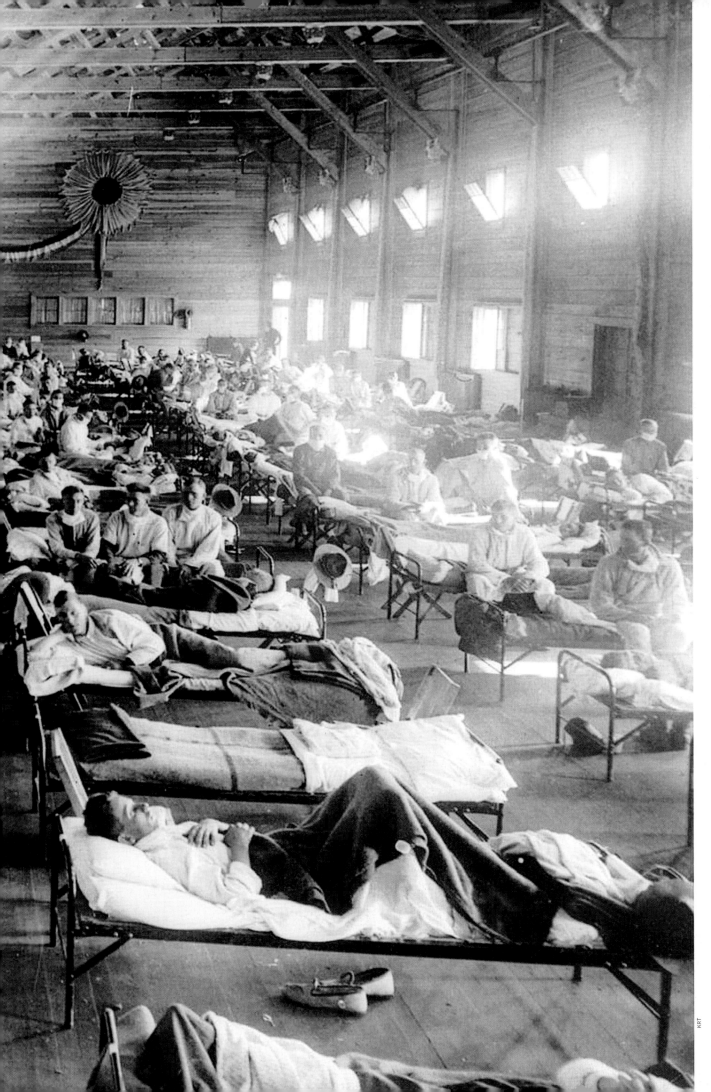

The Great Pandemic • 1918-19

Largely forgotten today, the influenza epidemic of 1918-19 was a calamity of global proportions. It remains the single most deadly pandemic of modern times: an estimated 650,000 Americans succumbed to the disease—four times the number of U.S. troops who died in World War I—and the influenza is believed to have killed 40 million to 60 million people around the planet.

The disease was widely called the Spanish Flu, but the term is a misnomer; the epidemic did not originate in Spain. The deadly ailment first struck the U.S. on March, 11, 1918, at Camp Funston at Fort Riley, outside Manhattan, Kans., when an Army private reported to the camp hospital just before breakfast complaining of fever, sore throat and headache. He was quickly followed by another soldier with similar complaints. By noon, the camp's hospital had dealt with more than 100 ailing soldiers. Indeed, the rapidity with which the disease spread and claimed victims was its most striking feature: people who felt well in the morning could become sick by noon and were dead by nightfall. In the picture at left, stricken soldiers fill a hospital ward at Camp Funston in 1918.

The flu ravaged America in two distinct periods, the first in the summer of 1918 and the second in the spring of 1919. As many as one-quarter of Americans are believed to have contracted the illness. After the second wave subsided, the Spanish Flu disappeared—as quickly and mysteriously as it had first emerged.

155

156

"The uncertainties of 1919 were over ... America was going on the greatest, gaudiest spree in history and there was going to be plenty to tell about it."

—F. SCOTT FITZGERALD, *THE CRACK-UP*

1919-29

All Jazzed Up

EVEN WHEN VIEWED FROM EIGHT DECADES IN THE FUTURE, THE 1920S CARRY A SPECIFIC SENSORY CHARGE: THE WHIFF OF bootleg gin, the sight of flappers dancing the Charleston, the din of voices cheering Babe Ruth and Charles Lindbergh. And as for the roar in the Roaring Twenties, it was provided by Louis Armstrong's jaunty trumpet. Ironically, the engine driving this feistiest of American eras was a social policy intended to promote calm. But the prohibition of alcohol that became the law of the land under the 18th Amendment in 1920 only made liquor, now a forbidden fruit, all the more alluring.

Fueled by exciting new media technologies (and bathtub gin), American life seemed to speed up in the 1920s, as buttons gave way to newfangled "zippers," and young women traded in corsets for "scanties." As poet Ezra Pound declared, "The age demanded an image of its accelerated grimace." And Americans found such images on every side; in an era that worshipped speed and exuberance, audiences laughed at the frantic comedy antics of the Keystone Kops and the Marx Brothers and reveled in the fascinating rhythms of George Gershwin, above, whose propulsive drive made the elegant syncopations of the ragtime era seem quaint.

158

Prohibition and the Law of Unintended Consequences

The movement to prohibit alcohol in the U.S. gained steam in the late 1800s, often marching in lockstep with the campaign for women's rights and suffrage, for alcohol abuse often led to domestic abuse.

But when Prohibition became the law of the land in 1920 under the 18th Amendment to the Constitution, its effect was precisely the opposite of its intent. Americans became bedazzled with the allure of the forbidden substance, and the law was widely flouted. A shady, thrillingly illicit culture of speakeasies, home brewers and bootleggers soon sprouted in the nation's cities. At right, Philadelphia public safety director "Duckboard" Butler dispatches illegal beer into the Schuylkill River in 1924.

With both the police and the judiciary corrupted by payoffs, with drunkenness rampant, criminal gangs proliferating and respect for the law declining, the hated, failed policy was finally repealed under the 21st Amendment in 1933.

SOCIAL TENSIONS BREED SCANDAL AND CRIME

Ethnic and racial tensions rocked the U.S. in the 1920s, as a revived Ku Klux Klan flourished, and lynchings kept Southern and Midwestern blacks suppressed. Radio and newsreels turned local trials into national sensations

Justice on Trial

Prejudice against the increasing number of immigrants arriving in the U.S. from southern Europe led to a 1924 law that favored northern Europeans. The 1921 conviction for murder of Italian immigrants Nicola Sacco, below right, and Bartolomeo Vanzetti, on scant evidence, sparked years of protest. They were executed in 1927.

The Law of the Noose

Inspired in part by the 1915 film *Birth of a Nation,* the Ku Klux Klan returned to life in the 1920s, attracting 3 million members to its anti–black, anti–immigrant, anti–Roman Catholic views. Twenty-three blacks were lynched in 1926 alone (above, two murders in Indiana), but anti-lynching legislation was blocked by Southern Democrats in the Senate. Hundreds more blacks died in race riots in Oklahoma and Florida.

A Mob Massacre in Chicago

Flourishing under Prohibition, gangsters ruled the streets of Chicago in the 1920s, turning the city into a worldwide byword for lawlessness. No one was convicted in the St. Valentine's Day Massacre of 1929, above, in which seven people were killed.

Evolution Takes the Stand

In the 1925 "Scopes monkey trial," which was nationally broadcast on radio, famed advocates Clarence Darrow, top, and William Jennings Bryan fought over the fate of teacher John Scopes, who defied the state law of Tennessee by teaching the theory of evolution; he was found guilty.

Bryan, the populist Democratic icon who ran for the presidency three times and later served as Secretary of State under Woodrow Wilson, became a hero to Christian Fundamentalists in the trial, but he died only five days after the verdict was returned.

A New Medium Combines Vast Reach with Surprising Intimacy

Although the technical advances that united performers in a Schenectady, N.Y., studio, left, with an Oregon farm family, right, were essentially complete before 1910, radio's commercial development was put on hold by World War I. But it resumed in earnest in the 1920s, driven by the exploding demand of a fascinated public. In 1922 there were only 30 radio stations operating in the U.S.; by 1923 there were 556. Radio became a truly mass medium with the founding of two coast-to-coast networks, the National Broadcasting Corp. in 1926 and the Columbia Broadcasting System in 1927. By 1933, two-thirds of all American homes had at least one radio. To signify their status, many radios in the '20s featured wood finishes and "cathedral" styling, right.

The new parlor companion united Americans in a new way: when President Franklin D. Roosevelt gave his series of "fireside chats" in the 1930s, he was employing a young medium to create a new, uniquely personal relationship with his constituents.

In an Exuberant Era, Artists Make Spectacles of Themselves

Movies and radio attracted huge audiences in the 1920s, but even so, live entertainment enjoyed a Golden Age. Magician and escape artist Harry Houdini was vastly popular; the vaudeville circuit flourished; and Broadway musicals proliferated, peaking in the great 1927 hit *Show Boat,* right. Writer F. Scott Fitzgerald and his wife and muse Zelda, center, were the cultural avatars of the jazz age.

A Renaissance in Harlem and All That Jazz

In the first decades of the century, thousands of Southern blacks migrated north in search of opportunity. By the 1920s, New York City's black district, Harlem, was the capital of African-American urban culture, and a generation of gifted artists, musicians and writers enjoyed an outpouring of creativity dubbed the Harlem Renaissance. Breaking through social taboos that had long divided the races, whites trouped to Harlem to enjoy the artistry of great black musicians and performers—no longer presented in the mocking, cartoonish spirit of the minstrel show, but with a newfound pride in black identity. Above, a chorus line performs at Harlem's famed jazz venue, the Cotton Club.

The soundtrack of the 1920s was a thrilling new musical form, jazz, which swept from its birthplace, New Orleans on the Gulf Coast, to win worldwide popularity. Upbeat, playful and flourishing on improvisation, jazz celebrated both individual virtuosity and the joys of group interplay. The propulsive, bubbling rhythms of the new sound mirrored the rapid-fire spirit of the times, and jazz became one of the great artistic exports of the U.S.; it has often been described as the nation's most prominent original contribution to world culture. At right, King Oliver's Creole Jazz Band starred a young Louis Armstrong, with trumpet in center. The New Orleans native, an international superstar for five decades, became America's foremost ambassador for jazz.

The Movies Head West

The film industry's first home in America was the nation's financial capital and the home of its largest audience, New York City. But in 1910 the Biograph Co. dispatched director D.W. Griffith and a troupe of stars to Los Angeles to make movies, attracted by the region's famously sunny climate, perfect for shooting outdoor scenes. The film industry gradually migrated to a small suburb of Los Angeles, Hollywood—where real estate speculators erected a sign with 50-ft. letters in 1923 to attract home buyers, above (the sign's final four letters were removed in 1945).

Hollywood's surge to become the world's film capital was explosive: by the 1920s, studios in Southern California were producing more than 800 feature films a year, some 80% of the global total. Hollywood's ascendance was aided by World War I, which crippled film industries abroad. The movies' biggest star was the British-born comedy genius Charlie Chaplin, whose fictional "Little Tramp" persona was perhaps the single most famous face on the planet.

TOP: BRUCE TORRENCE COLLECTION; LEFT: EVERETT COLLECTION

Fast Forward: The Movies Learn to Speak

Driven by a seemingly insatiable public appetite for the movies—the very name carries the abrupt zip of the era when it was coined—film production and technology developed rapidly. At left above, pioneering director D.W. Griffith shoots *The Escape* in 1914, using a single camera operator. Only 13 years later, during the shooting of *No Place to Go* in 1927, a multiperson camera and lighting crew, as well as director Mervyn LeRoy (in chair), are shooting scenes from a movable platform whose camera height can be moved up or down, while the background set is far more elaborate.

Film technology took its largest step forward when the movies became "talkies" with the development of sychronized sound. Warner Bros.' pioneering *The Jazz Singer* (1927), was largely silent but included sound during certain scenes, while the first widely seen animated film short with sound, Walt Disney's *Steamboat Willie* (1928), catapulted the cartoon rodent Mickey Mouse and his creator to worldwide fame.

163

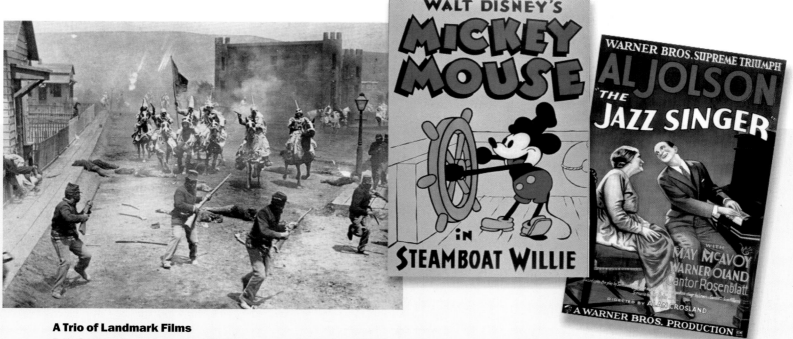

A Trio of Landmark Films

D.W. Griffith's *Birth of a Nation* (1915), above, was the first great Hollywood epic: the first film to run longer than an hour featured such relative novelties as the close-up and jump-cut. But advances in movie technology outpaced social mores: in *The Jazz Singer* Al Jolson performed in blackface, while *Birth of a Nation* glorified the exploits of the Ku Klux Klan during Reconstruction in the South.

Lucky Lindy, Spirit of an Ascending Age • 1927

The frenzied giddiness of the 1920s—stoked by the steady proliferation of mass media—reached an apex with the historic solo flight across the Atlantic made by aviator Charles Lindbergh in 1927, when he was only 25. The heroic traverse made the handsome pilot an instant American icon (and TIME's first Man of the Year). Lindbergh represented everything Americans wanted to believe about themselves: this nation, still a relative newcomer on the world stage, would harness technology to explore new frontiers. Below, a huge crowd gathers in London to hail Lindbergh and his single-engine *Spirit of St. Louis* days after the thrilling solo flight.

ON THE PLAYING FIELD, REVOLUTIONARY TECHNOLOGIES CREATE POPULAR STARS

In the 1920s new forms of communication—including radio and movie newsreels—created a national audience for athletes who previously might have been local heroes, and a new pantheon of stars made sports more popular than ever before

Red Grange

The celebrated running back gained national fame as a student at the University of Illinois, in the great heyday of college football. Turning pro and barnstorming for George Halas' Chicago Bears, the "Galloping Ghost" helped bring legitimacy to the fledgling National Football League.

Babe Ruth

Pudgy, pigeon-toed, moon-faced and irresistible to kids, Ruth broke into baseball as a dominating pitcher, but he turned himself into a slugger, solidifying baseball's claim to being the national pastime and making the home run the game's signature play. Everything about the jovial, larger-than-life New York Yankee was in tune with the '20s: his outsized exploits and appetites made ideal fodder for New York City's 10 daily newspapers.

Jack Dempsey

At a time when boxing was highly popular, Dempsey (seen here slugging Gene Tunney in 1927) was the Babe Ruth of the ring, a raffish, colorful, wealthy and widely beloved playboy.

Bobby Jones

The gifted amateur from Georgia made golf, a game once reserved for the rich, a sport for the masses. Jones helped found the Masters Tournament, still one of the game's premier championships.

1929-41

Down and Out

THE GIDDY GAIETY OF THE 1920S WAS DRIVEN IN PART BY THE STEADILY ASCENDING PRICES on America's stock exchanges. But the age of irrational exuberance ended when the markets crashed in October 1929, bringing the U.S. economy down with them. With stunning swiftness, the nation was transformed: in the worst economic calamity in U.S. history, 5,000 banks failed over a period of three years, erasing the life savings of millions. Farms and homes were lost; unemployment, poverty and hunger stalked the land. By one estimate, $30 billion of inflated stock value vanished into thin air in less than one month in 1929. Total farm income, as high as $15.5 billion in 1920, fell to $5 billion in 1933, by which time one of every three Americans was either unemployed or lived in a household whose breadwinner had no job.

When devastating dust storms began ravaging the Great Plains, as shown in this picture of a cloud descending on Boise City, Okla., in 1935, it seemed that America's long run as a land of opportunity and the birthplace of mankind's future was over. The White House and the citizens seemed helpless, uncertain, afraid—until a robust new President warned Americans that the enemy most to be feared was fear itself, and put them back to work.

"Once I built a tower, up to the sun, brick and rivet and lime
Once I built a tower, now it's done. Brother, can you spare a dime?

—E.Y. HARBURG, *BROTHER, CAN YOU SPARE A DIME?*

An Ailing, Depressed Democracy

In the face of the economic calamity unleashed by the stock-market crash of '29, President Herbert Hoover waited for market forces to correct the downturn; they did not. By the early 1930s, unemployed homeless people were living in jerry-built shantytowns dubbed "Hoovervilles," like the one in New York City at far right. Kitchens run by charities helped keep people alive; above, a bread line in New York City; at left, a soup kitchen in Washington.

Investors who rushed to banks to withdraw their savings, like the crowd at near right in New York City in 1931, only accelerated bank failures. In a country with millions out of work, some areas were especially hard hit: in Ohio, jobless rates reached 50% in Cleveland, 60% in Akron, 80% in Toledo. The woes persisted: despite a host of energetic federal New Deal programs, in 1937, eight years after the Crash of 1929, President Franklin D. Roosevelt declared, "I see one-third of a nation ill-housed, ill-clad, ill-nourished."

BETTMANN CORBIS

NEWS PHOTO

170

American Refugees

The great dust storms of the 1930s made nature seem malicious, for they turned the soil that had promised rich harvests into a dusty enemy that drove families from their homes. Novelist John Steinbeck indelibly portrayed the feel of the storms in the first chapter of *The Grapes of Wrath:*

"Little by little the sky was darkened by the mixing dust, and carried away. The wind grew stronger. The rain crust broke and the dust lifted up out of the fields and drove gray plumes into the air like sluggish smoke. The corn threshed the wind and made a dry, rushing sound. The finest dust did not settle back to earth now, but disappeared into the darkening sky ... The people came out of their houses and smelled the hot stinging air and covered their noses from it ... Men stood by their fences and looked at the ruined corn, drying fast now, only a little green showing through the film of dust. The men were silent and they did not move often. And the women came out of the houses to stand beside their men—to feel whether this time the men would break."

The "black blizzards" didn't break the men: they sent them on the road to seek work. New Deal photographer Dorothea Lange caught up with refugees Frances Owens Thompson and her children at a makeshift camp in Nipomo, Calif., in 1936 and captured their plight in a classic series of photographs. The image at left, if less familiar than others in the series, is equally moving.

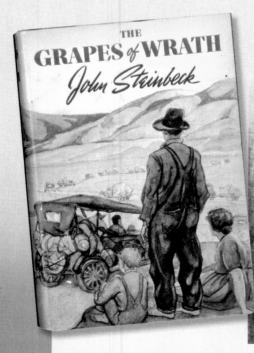

The Dust Bowl in Song and Story

The hardships and heroism of the Dust Bowl were chronicled in John Steinbeck's 1939 novel *The Grapes of Wrath.* LIFE magazine's Horace Bristol photographed the woman above in a California refugee camp while researching the lives of the Okies with Steinbeck. He did not record her name, but claimed she was the model for Steinbeck's stoic matriarch, Ma Joad.

Troubadour Woody Guthrie, right, traveled with the Okies and expressed their struggles in such anthems as *Do-Re-Mi:* "California is a garden of Eden/ A paradise to live in or see/ But believe it or not, you won't find it so hot/ If you ain't go the do-re-mi.

Uprooted and Heading West

In the Dust Bowl states—Oklahoma, Texas, Kansas, Colorado and New Mexico—an estimated 60% of the residents were driven from their homes in the mid-1930s to seek jobs and refuge. Whatever their home state, these "exodusters" were universally known as Okies, Oklahomans. Many of the displaced headed west toward the Golden State, California, where authorities eventually resorted to posting armed guards at the state line to keep out the indigent. This page records the progression of the refugees: below, a farmer and his children survey their ruined farm in Cimarron County, Okla., in 1936. Above, Okies hit the road, and unemployed workers seek welfare relief at a federal office in California.

New Deal, New Dollars, New Dams

Surveying an impoverished, exhausted nation two months after taking office in 1933, President Franklin D. Roosevelt attacked the Federal Government's passivity. "This country demands bold, persistent experimentation," he told Americans. "Take a method and try it. If it fails, admit it frankly and try another. But above all, try something."

Promising citizens a "New Deal" with their government, F.D.R. immediately began carving out a much more active role for Washington in the daily lives of Americans. Soon an alphabet soup of 59 new federal agencies—including the NRA (National Recovery Administration), WPA (Works Progress Administration) and CCC (Civilian Conservation Corps)—was putting the unemployed back to work. Critics charged F.D.R. with practicing socialism—the 1935 Social Security program was especially scorned by some Americans—but supporters said he was saving the economy with such major public-works projects as the Tennessee Valley Authority and the Fort Peck Dam on the Missouri River in Montana. Below, workers craft a turbine for the big Montana dam in 1936.

172

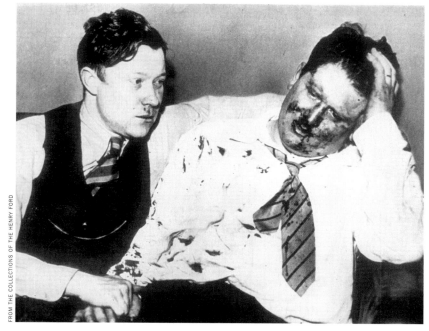

In a Desperate Era, Desperate Measures • 1937

The hard times of the 1930s soured some Americans on the capitalist system, and many on the left advocated socialism's state-run economies as a cure for the nation's woes; the period was a high-water mark for socialism in the U.S.

Lean times also pitted workers against owners, most famously in Detroit, where the leaders of the striking United Auto Workers, Walter Reuther, left, and Richard Frankensteen, were beaten by thugs hired by Ford Motor in 1937.

173

Working for Uncle Sam

President Roosevelt understood that the millions of workers standing idle in the nation were a recipe for social upheaval. The New Deal solution: put them to work in federal projects that improved their communities.

Above, Civilian Conservation Corps workers dig ditches in 1937. When the U.S. Supreme Court ruled that some New Deal programs were unconstitutional, F.D.R.'s plan to enlarge the court, stacking it in his favor, failed.

CCC Poster, 1933

In New Deal days, the government became a patron of the arts, funding plays, books and posters.

Encouraging Words

A voice of assurance when Americans most needed it, President Franklin D. Roosevelt solidified his ties with ordinary Americans with his groundbreaking series of plainspoken "fireside chats" on the radio. Above, F.D.R. delivers the first address on March 12, 1933. Elected to four terms in office, the longest-serving President came to seem synonymous with the nation, but future Presidents were barred from being elected more than twice by the 22nd Amendment of 1951.

IN A DEAD-END ERA, CRIMINALS BECOME CELEBRITIES

In normal times, bank robbers and murderers would be objects of scorn, but in the '30s, they were often portrayed as populist Robin Hoods battling a heartless system stacked against the "little guy"—while providing voyeuristic thrills in their battles with lawmen

Choose One: Public Enemies or Relentless "G-Men"

Below, the dapper robbers: from left, Charles (Pretty Boy) Floyd in 1930; Bonnie Parker and Clyde Barrow in 1930; and John Dillinger in 1933. Above, the cops: J. Edgar Hoover, the celebrated, publicity-loving head of the Federal Bureau of Investigation (FBI) is on right; at left is an FBI agent. Besotted with charismatic gangsters, Americans tuned into *Gangbusters* on the radio and loved square-jawed Dick Tracy in the comics.

Catastrophe in New Jersey • 1937

Symbol of a luckless era, the German zeppelin *Hindenburg*, heavily touted as the future of luxury transatlantic travel, caught fire and crashed while landing in New Jersey on May 6, 1937, killing 36 people. The disaster effectively put an end to the research and development of lighter-than-air craft for travel and commerce.

175

A Pioneer's Final Flight • 1937

In the 1930s aviation was still a novelty enjoyed by only a few; the first real airline service began in 1925. Aviator Amelia Earhart, above in 1937, captured American hearts and embodied women's dreams with a thrilling series of historic flights. Her disappearance while flying over the South Pacific that year sparked widespread grief— and decades of speculation.

Escape into Fantasy Lands

In a hard-times era, two fanciful 1939 movies, *Gone With the Wind* and *The Wizard of Oz,* became classics, while *Monopoly*, released in 1935, gave homebound families on a tight budget a chance to dream of real estate riches.

"With confidence in our armed forces, with the unbounding determination of our people, we will gain the inevitable triumph, so help us God."

—FRANKLIN D. ROOSEVELT, DEC. 8, 1941

Trials and Triumphs

THE STORM CLOUDS OF WAR HAD BEEN GATHERING FOR YEARS: JAPAN, LED by militant imperialists, attacked China in 1937; Germany, roused by Adolf Hitler's racist, totalitarian Nazi Party, absorbed Austria and part of Czechoslovakia in 1938. On Sept. 1, 1939, Hitler invaded Poland, plunging Europe into full-scale war. By 1940 the Japanese had allied themselves with Germany and were attacking Britain's colonial holdings across Asia, even as Nazi troops occupied Denmark, Norway, Holland, Belgium and France and laid siege to Britain. In 1941, a Hitler swollen with hubris double-crossed his fellow dictator and supposed ally, Joseph Stalin, and invaded the Soviet Union.

Yet as Europe and Asia burned, America remained serenely peaceful, seemingly protected from harm by two vast oceans. Fearing a major war, isolationists in Congress passed the Neutrality Act of 1937, forbidding President Franklin D. Roosevelt to aid either side. Roosevelt, well aware of the threat from Germany and Japan, had begun quietly preparing America for the coming conflict; his "Lend-Lease" policy of 1940 sent ships and arms to Britain. It took the devastating shock of Japan's Dec. 7, 1941, surprise attack on Pearl Harbor, the U.S. naval base in Hawaii, to rouse a sleeping nation from its torpor, as 2,403 Americans lost their lives. Here, Japanese bombs set the battleships U.S.S. *West Virginia* and U.S.S. *Tennessee* afire; both were repaired and returned to service later in the war.

D-Day: The Allies Strike Back • 1944

When Nazi Germany declared war on the U.S. in December 1941, citing America's alliance with Japan, Adolf Hitler was the master of Europe. As Britain struggled to survive, the swastika flag flew over most of the Continent and much of Hitler's former ally, Russia, while vassal states (such as Vichy France), allies (like dictator Benito Mussolini's Italy) and sympathizers (like Francisco Franco's Spain) controlled much of the rest.

The U.S. effort on the Western Front began slowly, with green G.I.s fighting the Germans in northern Africa, then landing in Sicily and later battling German and Italian armies up the Italian peninsula. By the spring of 1944, the U.S. and its Allies were finally prepared to launch an offensive on Hitler's Western Front, in hopes of wresting occupied France from Germany's grip.

General Dwight D. Eisenhower's Order of the Day for June 6, 1944 began, "Soldiers, Sailors and Airmen of the Allied Expeditionary Forces: You are about to embark upon the Great Crusade, toward which we have striven these many months." With these words, "Ike," the top Allied general, dispatched the largest sea-borne invasion force ever assembled from Britain across the English Channel.

Facing a desperate, entrenched enemy, on "D-day," American and Allied soldiers jumped from airplanes, sprinted up beaches, scaled cliffs and stormed bunkers to beat back the German defenders positioned along Hitler's Atlantic Wall. The cost of their valor was staggering: in the first 24 hours, some 10,000 Allied troops were killed, while another 40,000 fell in the following days. Yet the invaders succeeded in their mission, establishing a secure foothold along a 40-mile stretch of beach on the Normandy Coast.

This photo, taken on June 8, or "D-plus-two," gives some sense of the scale of the operation, as Allied ships land supplies and fresh troops at the scene of some of the heaviest fighting on D-day, Omaha Beach. By D-plus-six, a week after the invasion, the Allies had landed more than 326,000 troops, 50,000 vehicles and 100,000 tons of supplies. Within 90 days, Allied armies would march in triumph into Paris. Within a year, both Hitler and his 1,000 Year Reich would be dead.

179

180

Victory in Europe • 1944-45

The successful U.S.-led invasion of occupied France on D-day sealed the fate of Hitler's Third Reich. During the summer of 1994, U.S. and Allied troops under generals including Dwight Eisenhower and the hard-driving George Patton, top right, sent German forces reeling backward across northern Europe. In December 1944, Hitler launched a final, desperate attempt to contain the Allied armies advancing on Germany. Martialing their troops with precision, the Germans succeeded in utterly surprising the Allies with a counterattack that began on Dec. 16. The gambit worked, as the Germans pushed the troops backwards, creating a bulge in the Allied lines. But U.S. soldiers dug in, fighting from foxholes, above right, and amid the deep snows of Belgium, right page, and the Battle of the Bulge turned out to be Germany's last offensive on the Western Front.

As Allied armies marched into Hitler's empire in the spring of 1945, the full extent of his evil was revealed, as prisoners were liberated from hundreds of concentration camps and death factories, including Buchenwald, right. Amid such horrors, G.I. cartoonist Bill Mauldin provided a welcome dose of humor with his portrayals of the lives of everyday soldiers in the U.S. Army newspaper *Stars and Stripes*, above.

182

America's War in the Pacific • 1942-45

In the days after Pearl Harbor, the U.S. faced daunting odds in the Far East. Most of the Pacific fleet was severely damaged, but in a stroke of luck, America's aircraft carriers had been out to sea when the Japanese struck the naval base. They became the linchpin of a campaign that deployed carrier-launched airplanes to support a hopscotch strategy of amphibious island invasions. The May 1942 Battle of the Coral Sea was technically a draw, but it halted the Japanese juggernaut. In the Battle of Midway four weeks later, the Japanese took a beating, losing four carriers and hundreds of their best pilots (above, U.S. sailors on the sinking carrier U.S.S. *Yorktown* in that battle). In August the Allies began their first offensive with an amphibious landing on Guadalcanal. Three years of bloody fighting followed as U.S. troops landed on islands like Tarawa, Saipan and Guam (where USO dancers entertained U.S. sailors in 1945, left). Finally, in July 1945 the U.S. recaptured the Philippines.

Closer to Japan, thousands of lives were lost on both sides on the islands of Iwo Jima and Okinawa in 1945, as the entrenched Japanese fought to the death. Above left, U.S. troops land on the island. By August of 1945, the invasion of Japan loomed. U.S. generals estimated that the battle to take control of the enemy's homeland would claim the lives of 1 million Americans and far more Japanese.

Raising the Stars and Stripes on Mount Suribachi • 1945

In the Pacific, American determination and Japanese ferocity peaked in the battle for the 8-sq.-mi. volcanic island south of Japan called Iwo Jima. In the month-long conflict that began on Feb. 19, 1945, the casualty rate suffered by U.S. Marines was the highest in American history, while more than 98% of the 20,000 dug-in Japanese troops died. Four days into the campaign, Marines reached the summit of Mount Suribachi, the island's highest point, where they raised an American flag to boost the morale of troops fighting on the beaches 500 ft. below. When that flag proved too small to see from a distance, five Marines and a Navy medic set out to hoist a larger flag on the summit.

The second flag raising was seen around the world, thanks to Associated Press photographer Joe Rosenthal, who snapped the action at a key moment. (The photo, contrary to some accounts, was not staged.) The dynamic image electrified Americans' morale. Sadly, it didn't mark the end of the battle: three of the six men in the photo were killed within days. Rosenthal died 61 years after taking the photograph, in August 2006. At right, the two flags are swapped.

The Home Front: "Don't You Know There's a War On?"

The great two-front, four-year war transformed American society: thousands of women worked in defense plants, while citizens rallied to buy bonds, recycle tires and other goods or serve as civil defense volunteers. The sense of national unity and shared sacrifice that had helped Americans endure the Depression era was now devoted to the war effort. A rare blot on America's wartime conduct was the confining of some 120,000 Japanese Americans in detention camps; the women at right are at Heart Mountain in Wyoming in 1943.

The Art of Winning the War

Wartime posters saluted women workers, promoted war bonds and urged Americans to grow their own food so more could go to soldiers. The government issued ration books and token "points," right, to allocate food and gas.

BLACK STARS BEGIN TO LEVEL THE PLAYING FIELD IN AMERICAN SPORTS

While black U.S. soldiers were winning respect for their service in World War II, African-American athletes in the U.S. were staking their claim to stardom. Their success helped lead the way toward the end of segregation in America

Joe Louis

Americans of all races who loved his class and clout called Detroit's Louis "the Brown Bomber." The heavyweight, here seen knocking out Willy Conn in 1946, thrilled the world when he defeated German Max Schmeling (who was unfairly portrayed as a Nazi sympathizer) in 1938.

Satchel Paige

The ageless pitcher, at left playing in the Negro Leagues in 1941, is considered one of the greatest hurlers of all time, but segregation kept him out of the big leagues until 1948, when he was past his prime. An engaging showoff and champion boaster, Paige bragged that his rules for staying young included "Avoid running at all times" and "Don't look back—something might be gaining on you."

Sugar Ray Robinson

The thoughtful middleweight with the fleet feet and potent punch was a popular figure in the years after World War II, especially in Harlem, where he showed off his restaurant and his Cadillac in 1950.

Jackie Robinson

Brooklyn Dodgers owner Branch Rickey and his star infielder integrated baseball in 1947, after Robinson played in Montreal. The two men were reviled by some, but their courage is now acclaimed.

Age of Anxiety

AS AMERICAN SOLDIERS BATTLED JAPAN IN 1945 IN A MEAT-GRINDER CAMPAIGN of amphibious island invasions, U.S. physicists worked frantically to create a weapon based on their new insights into nuclear power. They succeeded: at right, the atom bomb is tested for the first time, on July 16, 1945. Within weeks, President Harry Truman ordered the bomb to be dropped on two Japanese cities, Hiroshima and Nagasaki. Both were devastated: more than 200,000 civilians were killed, and Japan soon surrendered. Truman argued that in the long run the bombings saved lives on both sides, making a bloody Allied invasion of Japan unnecessary.

The twin blasts marked the end of the great two-front war, which TIME christened World War II. But they also marked the beginning of a new conflict. The two nations that emerged from the battlefields as new world powers were the U.S. and the Soviet Union—and their worldviews were deeply antithetical. A long struggle, soon dubbed the cold war, ensued. But the farsighted plans put in place by U.S. statesmen soon after World War II—the policy of "containment" of Soviet expansion, the North Atlantic Treaty Organization, the United Nations, the new World Bank and the Marshall Plan that rebuilt shattered Europe—laid the foundation for America's eventual triumph. At home, though, Americans who had every right to celebrate their magnificent victory in World War II found themselves apprehensive instead, haunted by fears of a nuclear holocaust and communist aggression.

"A shadow has fallen upon the scenes so lately lighted by the Allied victory. Nobody knows what Soviet Russia and its communist international organization intends to do in the immediate future, or what are the limits, if any, to their expansive and proselytizing tendencies."

—WINSTON CHURCHILL, "IRON CURTAIN" SPEECH, MARCH 5, 1946

Airlift to Berlin • 1948-49

World War II in Europe concluded with Germany's surrender in May 1945. But a new contest between the war's two greatest victors, the U.S. and the Soviet Union, quickly began, focusing on the ruined Nazi capital of Berlin. With Germany divided between the former allies and partitioned Berlin located deep in Soviet-controlled eastern Germany, communist leader Joseph Stalin tested the resolve of the U.S. and its European allies by blocking off the roadways leading to Berlin on June 24, 1948. The Western allies responded with the Berlin Airlift, thwarting Stalin by sending essential supplies into the isolated city via a flotilla of aircraft, with more than 275,000 flights taking place over a 321-day period.

A Bitter Stalemate on the Korean Peninsula • 1950-53

In 1949, communist leader Mao Zedong seized control of China, Asia's giant, impoverished power. The new alliance between Beijing and Moscow dismayed Americans, and their fears of communist expansion were realized on June 25, 1950, when Chinese client state North Korea sent its troops across the 38th parallel, the postwar line drawn by diplomats across the Korean peninsula to denote areas of Soviet and U.S. influence. President Harry Truman quickly sent U.S. troops to aid South Korea under the auspices of the new international body the United Nations, and after initial defeats, a surprise Allied landing at Inchon sent the North Koreans into full retreat. But China entered the war in November 1950, after World War II hero General Douglas MacArthur sent U.S. troops close to China's borders. Mao's armies, with vastly superior numbers, sent U.S. troops reeling.

Truman fired MacArthur, and the war ground on for two more years, ending in a 1953 stalemate that still divides the peninsula. Above, left: U.S. Marines retreat in bitter weather in December 1950; at right, Pfc. Roman Prauty fires a 75-mm recoilless rifle in June 1951. Below, a column of U.S. troops move through a burning South Korean village the same year.

IN AN UNEASY ERA, FEARS OF COMMUNISM SPAWN PARANOIA—AND A HARMFUL "RED SCARE"

On Feb. 9, 1950, Senator Joseph McCarthy, without proof, charged that communist agents had infiltrated the U.S. State Department. As paranoia peaked, congressional inquisitors turned the spotlight on alleged conspirators in Hollywood in televised hearings

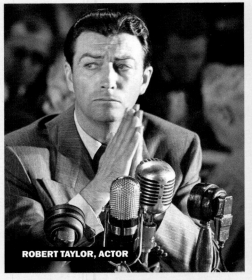

ROBERT TAYLOR, ACTOR

ADOLF MENJOU, ACTOR

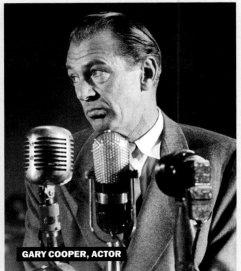

GARY COOPER, ACTOR

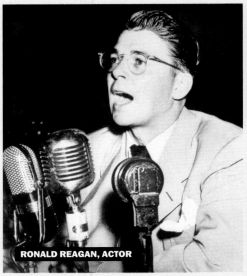

RONALD REAGAN, ACTOR

BERTHOLT BRECHT, PLAYWRIGHT

RING LARDNER JR., SCREENWRITER

190

In the Spotlight's Glare

Challenged by a little-understood enemy, international communism, many Americans fell victim to the fear-mongering tactics of a once-obscure Senator from Wisconsin, Joseph McCarthy, in the early 1950s. At near right, McCarthy consults with attorney Roy Cohn.

In his four-year reign of terror, McCarthy and his allies slandered public servants and led witch hunts that ruined the careers of U.S. diplomats and Hollywood figures, among other targets; above are some of those who testified in congressional hearings. Admired TV newsman Edward R. Murrow, far right, helped end the debacle with a forthright 1954 attack on McCarthy.

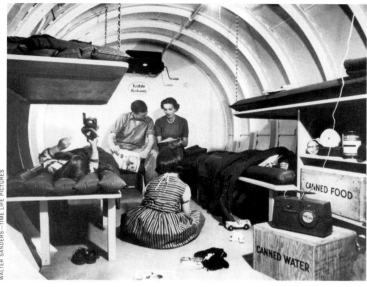

Duck and Cover!

Americans were stunned in 1953 when the Soviet Union exploded a nuclear bomb, achieving parity in the post–World War II arms race. The discovery that physicist Klaus Fuchs had turned over atom-bomb secrets to the Soviets only fed the "red scare" chill of the early 1950s. With the U.S. locked in an arms stalemate with the Soviets under the apocalyptic strategy of mutual assured destruction (its stunning acronym: MAD), American schoolkids were taught to "duck and cover," left—a pitifully ineffective defense against nuclear fallout. Some families built survivalist bomb shelters, as seen in a 1955 picture above.

191

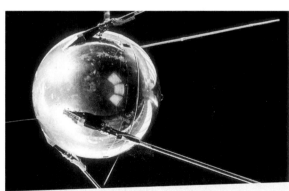

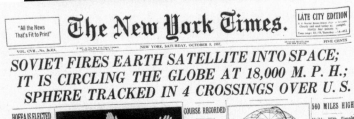

Sputnik Jump-Starts the Space Race

When the U.S.S.R. launched the first satellite in earth orbit, the 183-lb. Sputnik, on Oct. 4, 1957, Americans were shocked to find themselves trailing in the contest to explore a new frontier: space.

Vice President Nixon Debates Khrushchev in Russia · 1959

The U.S. and U.S.S.R. battled each other in the cold war through client nations, espionage and propaganda. After new Soviet boss Nikita Khrushchev criticized former leader Joseph Stalin at a 1956 party congress, a brief thaw saw Khrushchev engage in a spontaneous debate on economics with Vice President Richard Nixon at a 1959 Moscow trade show, above. Khrushchev toured the U.S. later that year. But when a U.S. U-2 spyplane was shot down over Russia in 1960, these halting attempts at rapprochement ended.

Age of Affluence

AFTER WORLD WAR II, AMERICANS MAY HAVE EMBRACED THEIR NATION'S NEW STATUS AS A GLOBAL superpower with some hesitation, but they welcomed with open arms the lengthy period of prosperity that victory brought. Returning soldiers and Americans whose lives had been disrupted by years of war and depression pursued long-entertained visions: of quiet normality, of comfort and security, of kids and pajamas and games of tag. One dream was new: cities began sprouting suburbs, gleaming magnets for middle-class aspiration. With a trusted authority figure, war hero Dwight D. Eisenhower, in the White House, Americans loved Lucy, argued about Elvis and agreed that *Father Knows Best*.

Free from war's yoke, the nation got back to doing what it does so well—inventing the future—as television and computers and a vast new interstate highway system remade the land. Yet beneath this apparent sea of tranquillity, change was bubbling. Almost 100 years after the Civil War, African Americans began demanding the right to be treated as equals. And those pajama-clad tykes, later christened the "baby boomers," would soon come of age: in the 1960s they would begin to wonder if father knew best, after all.

193

"The United States is the locomotive at the head of mankind, and the rest of the world the caboose." —DEAN ACHESON, U.S. SECRETARY OF STATE

Disney's Sanitized Kingdom • 1955

Walt Disney, the artist and visionary who helped pioneer animated films in the 1920s and '30s, achieved success by targeting his products specifically to young children and their parents. His celebrated string of early full-length animated films, including *Snow White and the Seven Dwarfs*, *Pinocchio* and *Bambi*, are technically innovative, classic works of art.

In the 1950s, Disney turned his genius to an institution badly in need of a makeover, the amusement park. Opening Disneyland, his "Magic Kingdom," in Anaheim, Calif., in 1955, Disney reinvented the form. His new "theme park"—like a modern-day Currier and Ives lithograph brought to life—reflected America's idealized image of itself, from the unwild West of Frontierland to the amiable, turn-of-the century Main Street U.S.A. to the future-besotted Tomorrowland.

Birth of the Cool

In the '50s, a new term from jazz musicians caught on: if you were cool—you were hot. Among the coolest of cats was actor James Dean, who lived fast and died young, in a car crash at age 24. At right, rock 'n' rollers hit Kansas in 1957.

THE INVENTION OF THE TEENAGER

With affluence building, college attendance rising, youngsters entering the work force later, new media emerging and companies targeting buyers more precisely, the 1950s gave birth to a new demographic group: teenagers

195

First Rumblings of a Coming Youthquake

The word teenager is a recent coinage; Teddy Roosevelt and Mark Twain never heard it. And that's the point: it wasn't until the postwar years that a distinctive culture based on adolescence developed in the U.S. And while styles have changed, the favored activities of these 1950s teens—gossiping, driving, dancing, dating and "hanging out"—have simply evolved: their 45 r.p.m. records are today's iPods; their phone chats are today's MySpace pages. (One exception: blue jeans never seem to go out of style.) At right is the perennially boyish TV host Dick Clark, broadcasting his long-running dance show, *American Bandstand,* in 1958.

196

Elvis Shakes, America Rattles, and Rock Gets Rolling

Memphis record producer Sam Phillips knew just what sort
of musician he was looking for in the mid-1950s: "a white man
who had a Negro sound and a Negro feel." That man, 18-year-
old Elvis Presley, walked into Phillips' Sun Records studio on
July 18, 1953, and recorded two songs to give to his mother as
a birthday gift. Almost a year later, an intrigued Phillips put
Presley into the studio with local musicians Scotty Moore and
Bill Black to see if sparks might fly. After a few uninspired
attempts at covering standard ballads, the band took a break. A
relaxed Presley picked up a guitar and began to play an upbeat
version of Arthur Crudup's blues tune *That's All Right, Mama*—
and Phillips had found the voice of his black-and-white dreams.

Presley didn't invent rock 'n' roll, but he popularized it; his
raucous, upbeat songs delighted the nation's teenagers and
dismayed their parents—a recipe for musical success that has
proved enduring. His dynamic moves in performance reflected
the raw energy of the new sound, whose powerful rhythms
were driven by an emphasis on the off-beat. "His entire
body takes on a frantic quiver, as if he had swallowed a jack-
hammer," TIME declared in 1956. "The sight and sound of him
drive teenage girls wild." Here, Elvis deploys his inspired
gyrations upon a swooning crowd of teens at a concert in
his hometown of Tupelo, Miss., in 1956.

Half a century after Presley and Phillips launched their
exuberant revolution, rock 'n' roll and its many offshoots
remain the most prominent vehicle for the passions, pleasures
and anxieties of American youth, with one welcome development: the artistry of black musicians no longer has to be
presented in a white package to reach a mainstream audience.

ROGER MARSHUTZ-MPTV

One Nation, Under the Sway of a Screen

Like two great change agents of technology that preceded it, the automobile and airplane, the arrival of television transformed the broad landscape of American life—and no one believes the revolutions of the video age are yet at an end. Television technology was just getting off the ground in the late 1930s, but the war years put a hold on its commercial rollout. As the new medium moved into homes rapidly in the early 1950s, it changed the way Americans entertained and informed themselves as well as the routines of family life, the conduct of politics and the marketing of products—all while making the nation's culture less regionally diverse and more homogeneous. Above, a sea of TVs takes up an entire sales floor in Chicago in 1956; below, a Little Rock, Ark., family gathers around the electronic hearth in 1953. One thing hasn't changed: we swear we hate TV, but we can't stop watching it.

Feeding Frenzy

Who's got time to cook— Milton Berle is coming on! Swanson helped change family life with the debut of the TV dinner in 1953, while the new medium spawned an enduring new magazine the same year.

Make Room—Lots of Room—for the Computer

These staid scenes don't appear to capture a revolution in progress, but in the whirring hum of room-filling electronic computers of the 1950s, one can hear the first stirrings of Google, YouTube and Wikipedia. Like so many 20th century technological advances, computer development was accelerated by the forced march of war, as World War II generals called on the big machines to plot ballistics, chart logistics and massage statistics.

Among the gizmo's pioneers was J.W. Mauchly, shown working above with the ENIAC (Electronic Numerical Integrator and Computer) machine in 1946. At left, a woman demonstrates Remington-Rand's UNIVAC (Universal Automatic Computer) in 1954. Computer technology was brought to the corporate marketplace in the 1950s by a number of firms; International Business Machines (IBM) became the industry's dominant force.

200

WILL COUNTS—ARKANSAS DEMOCRAT-GAZETTE

Fresh Battles for Black Rights

The fight for full civil rights for African Americans grew stronger in the mid-1950s. The U.S. Supreme Court helped advance the struggle when it issued a landmark ruling in the 1954 case *Brown v. Board of Education,* holding that segregated schools for blacks were not "separate but equal." When Rosa Parks, right, refused to give up her seat to a white man on a Montgomery, Ala., bus in 1955, the Rev. Martin Luther King Jr., far right, then 26, led a 382-day boycott that led to the integration of the bus lines.

In 1957 Arkansas Governor Orval Faubus and local whites challenged nine gutsy black youths who tried to integrate Little Rock's Central High School, above. President Dwight D. Eisenhower sent in U.S. Army troops to ensure the students were enrolled.

MONTGOMERY COUNTRY SHERIFF'S OFFICE

BETTMANN CORBIS

Herald of a Renaissance of Fundamentalist Christianity

Filling stadiums with impassioned believers, the Rev. Billy Graham thundered onto the American scene in the early 1950s bearing the message of repentance and salvation practiced by the muscular, Fundamentalist form of Christianity native to the South. Above, Graham speaks in Washington, in 1960. Tall, committed, commanding and a rousing speaker (TIME dubbed him "God's machine-gun"), Graham was the first Christian Evangelical to be welcomed into America's mainstream culture: predecessors like Billy Sunday had been seen by many as cranks or hucksters. In contrast, Graham's sincerity, humility and devotion to his calling—he led an exhausting series of revivals around the world—won wide respect, as fellow clergymen and Presidents sought his counsel and blessing.

Graham defied the values of many of his own followers, speaking out strongly for racial integration. His work helped create wide-spread new interest in Christian Fundamentalism, which would emerge as a major force in U.S. political life when Evangelicals began marshaling their energies to attack the 1973 legalization of abortion by the U.S. Supreme Court. In the last two decades of the century, conservative Christians would strongly condemn the changing cultural norms they regarded as harmful to U.S. moral values.

202

A Doyen of Ditz Dominates the Dial

Six months after *I Love Lucy* first appeared in America's living rooms on Oct. 15, 1951, it was the No. 1 show in the country—and the primary reason why TV sets, earlier a luxury purchase, now became a necessity. There's no mystery about the show's success: star Lucille Ball was a brilliant comedian, whose dithering-shrewd persona, bug-eyed double takes and nifty pratfalls have delighted generations of fans. Husband Desi Arnaz, who played a clueless Cuban bandleader onscreen, was in fact a TV innovator who filmed the shows with three cameras before a live audience—still the prevailing sitcom formula five decades later.

The Bad Cat Behind *Johnny B. Goode*

If Elvis Presley represented sanitized rock 'n' roll, Chuck Berry was the anti-Elvis. The slick-talking, duck-walking, self-proclaimed *Brown-Eyed Handsome Man* from St. Louis wrote joyous riffs that would be copped by the Beatles, the Rolling Stones, the Beach Boys and many others, while his speedy way with a lyric would later be ripped off by rappers.

A Golden Age of Musical Comedy

The distinctly American theatrical form dazzled as never before in the 1950s, as composers and lyricists pushed the form's limits, investing shows with Shavian wit, Midwestern nostalgia, urban tension and Oriental exoticism.

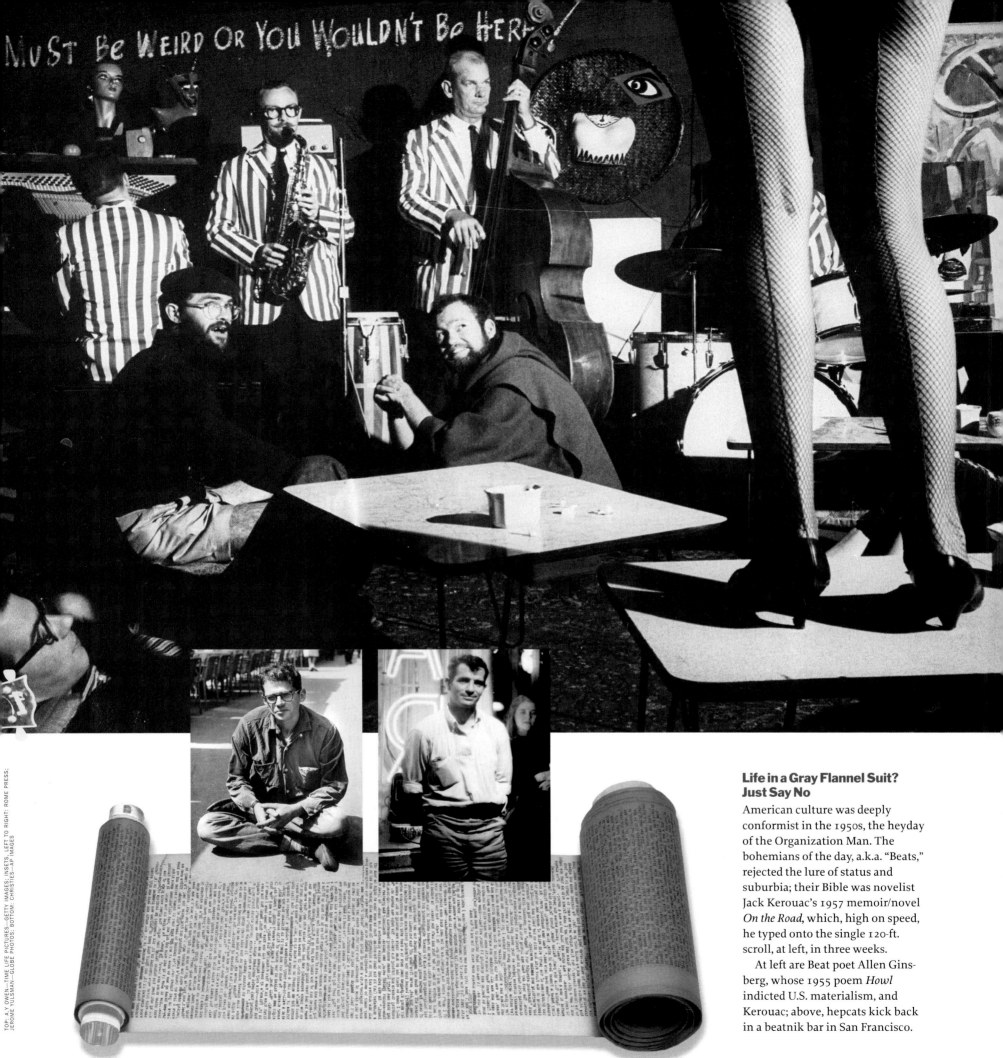

MUST BE WEIRD OR YOU WOULDN'T BE HERE

Life in a Gray Flannel Suit? Just Say No

American culture was deeply conformist in the 1950s, the heyday of the Organization Man. The bohemians of the day, a.k.a. "Beats," rejected the lure of status and suburbia; their Bible was novelist Jack Kerouac's 1957 memoir/novel *On the Road*, which, high on speed, he typed onto the single 120-ft. scroll, at left, in three weeks.

At left are Beat poet Allen Ginsberg, whose 1955 poem *Howl* indicted U.S. materialism, and Kerouac; above, hepcats kick back in a beatnik bar in San Francisco.

1960-69

Long Strange Trip

LIKE THE 1840S AND THE 1920S, THE 1960S WERE AN EXHILARATING, EXHAUSTING PERIOD IN AMERICAN history, an era of radical change when energies long bottled up crystallized into novel, even bizarre forms. In this period of polarization, there seemed to be no middle ground: America's division bell sounded, and everyone moved to the extremes, separating into young and old, hawks and doves, blacks and whites. Ironies abounded: revolutionary changes brought many more African Americans into the mainstream—even as inner-city blacks torched stores, homes and cars. A nation in love with the future landed the first men on the moon—even as young Americans died by the thousands in an ancient land, Vietnam, that was unfamiliar to many Americans before U.S. troops began serving there. And the U.S. economy hit new peaks of prosperity—even as college students rejected the values and aspirations of mainstream society. On the streets and campuses, skirts got shorter, hair got longer, music got louder. As the Grateful Dead sang, "What a long strange trip it's been." Just how strange? Take another look at that last sentence, and try imagining a musical group calling itself the Grateful Dead before the 1960s—much less the word trip being used to describe not a physical journey but rather an inner voyage fueled by the psychedelic drug LSD.

Come mothers and fathers/ Throughout the land/ And don't criticize/ What you can't understand/ Your sons and your daughters/ Are beyond your command/ ... For the times, they are a-changin.' —BOB DYLAN, *THE TIMES THEY ARE A-CHANGIN'*

PAUL SCHUTZER—TIME LIFE PICTURES

New Era, New Leader, New Frontiers · 1960

After the dowdy complacency of Dwight Eisenhower's 1950s, America was ready for a Chief Executive who would "get the country moving again," as Massachusetts Democrat John F. Kennedy promised to do during the 1960 presidential campaign. Fusing matinee-idol looks and a glamorous extended family, above, with war-hero toughness and a zestful, witty intelligence, Kennedy seemed to embody the best virtues America saw in itself at the hopeful dawn of a new decade. Reporters used the term charisma, then new to most Americans, to describe his appeal. The youngest man ever elected to the White House was also the first modern media candidate; his father, the wealthy Boston Irishman Joe Kennedy, had vowed, "We'll sell Jack like soap flakes." Kennedy's Roman Catholic faith was a major campaign issue, helping make his race with Richard Nixon one of the closest in U.S. history.

Once in office, J.F.K. and his young wife and family charmed the nation, while he tapped its can-do idealism with programs like the Peace Corps. The spirit of the times was embodied in a phrase from his acceptance speech at the 1960 Democratic Convention: "We stand at the edge of a New Frontier—the frontier of unfulfilled hopes and dreams."

THE U.S.-SOVIET DUEL ERUPTS ON TWO FRONTS

In his Inaugural Address, J.F.K. described the cold war struggle as nearing "the hour of maximum danger." His words soon proved prophetic, as the Soviets tested his resolve

The Bay of Pigs

In 1959 communist revolutionary Fidel Castro stunned Americans by toppling Cuba's corrupt, pro-U.S. leader, Fulgencio Batista. President Kennedy inherited an ill-considered Eisenhower Administration plan to land pro-U.S. exiles, left, in Cuba to spark an anti-Castro uprising. J.F.K. approved the plan, but the April 1961 invasion at the Bay of Pigs failed, in an utter fiasco. Only three months into his term, J.F.K. had to own up to a major foreign policy blunder.

207

The Berlin Wall

The most enduring symbol of cold war tensions—a wall that divided East and West Berlin and imprisoned half the city inside the communist sector—began rising at Soviet leader Nikita Khrushchev's command in August 1961. Although publicly outraged, Kennedy was privately relieved that the Wall, Winston Churchill's "iron curtain" vision realized in concrete and stone, removed Berlin as a flashpoint that might have ignited nuclear war.

Cuban Missile Crisis

Kennedy was told in October 1962 that the Soviets were arming Cuba with nuclear missiles. Resisting calls to bomb or invade the island, he opted for a naval blockade, right; the Russians backed down and removed the weapons. The price: the U.S. secretly removed its missiles from Turkey.

209

Horror Preserved on Film • 1963

The last words John F. Kennedy ever heard were uttered by Nellie Connally, the wife of Texas Governor John Connally, who was seated in front and to the left of the President as J.F.K. and his wife Jackie traveled through Dallas on a fence-mending political journey on Nov. 22, 1963. A few seconds after 12:30 p.m., Mrs. Connally turned to Kennedy and said, "You can't say Dallas doesn't love you, Mr. President." Her comment was followed by a sound similar to that of a firecracker—an event captured by Dallas clothing manufacturer Abraham Zapruder. Standing about 60 ft. away, Zapruder was taking a Super 8 film of Kennedy's motorcade. He caught 486 frames of the presidential limousine passing through Dealey Plaza.

In this frame from perhaps the most scrutinized and controversial set of images ever captured on film, Kennedy clutches his throat and leans forward after being hit for the first time. A few seconds later, another bullet impact, this one fatal, sent him reeling backward and to his left side. The seeming difference in the origin of the two shots has haunted America for more than four decades. A distinguished commission headed by Chief Justice of the U.S. Supreme Court Earl Warren identified Lee Harvey Oswald as the President's single assassin, but that did not convince the public: a 2003 ABC News poll found that 70% of Americans do not believe that Oswald acted alone.

Concerning the event's larger impact, no poll need be taken. For many Americans, a sense of national innocence was lost on that day and has yet to return.

History in a Heartbeat • 1963

John F. Kennedy was the first U.S. Chief Executive to be assassinated in office since William McKinley was shot and killed in 1901. For Americans who lived through the shocking experience, it was an act unmatched in horror until the terrorist attacks of Sept. 11, 2001. After Kennedy was pronounced dead in a Dallas hospital, Lyndon B. Johnson was sworn in as President aboard Air Force One; Jacqueline Kennedy, her coat still stained with her husband's blood, bore witness. The wild ride of the 1960s had begun.

Toward a Great Society

Lyndon Johnson, a man of big dreams and political skills to match them, set out to build on (and surpass) F.D.R.'s New Deal with the "Great Society." A master legislative tactician, Johnson persuaded Congress to enact a flurry of new laws that Kennedy could not, including the landmark Civil Rights Act of 1964, the Voting Rights Act of 1965 and the Medicare program of 1965. At right, L.B.J. visits poor kids in Kentucky in 1965; he declared a War on Poverty, but it was soon eclipsed by his other war, in Vietnam.

Full Speed Ahead, into a Quagmire in Southeast Asia

When Lyndon Johnson took office, he inherited a U.S. commitment to a little-known country in Southeast Asia divided, like Korea, into two nations. Communist North Vietnam, led by longtime anticolonial warrior Ho Chi Minh, was seeking to take over Western ally South Vietnam. When Johnson became President, there were some 20,000 U.S. troops in South Vietnam. Heeding standard cold war strategy, which stressed containing communism on every front to avoid a "domino effect" in which one nation's destiny would infect that of its neighbors, L.B.J. ramped up U.S. involvement. By 1968, more than 500,000 U.S. troops, most of them drafted, were in South Vietnam, and a massive bombing campaign was under way. Yet victory was nowhere in sight, and frustrated Americans began turning against the war. Protesters chanted, "Hey, hey, L.B.J.! How many kids did you kill today?"

At left, Johnson breaks down in 1968 while listening to a tape recording made by his son-in-law Captain Charles Robb, who spoke about his sorrow at losing young Americans under his command in battle. Stymied by the war, Johnson declared in March 1968 that he would not run for a second term.

THE WAR IN VIETNAM: DEATH IN LIVING COLOR

As the conflict in Vietnam dragged on for years, Americans became deeply divided over the rationale and conduct of the campaign, as, for the first time in the history of warfare, they watched the carnage of faraway battles in their living rooms on television

211

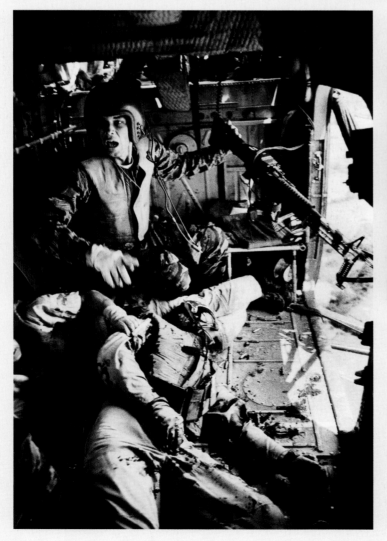

Postcards from Hell: Visions of Vietnam

By 1967, years into its effort to prop up the weak government of South Vietnam, the U.S. had dropped more tons of bombs against North Vietnam than the combined total it loosed on Germany and Japan during World War II. Yet it was Ho Chi Minh, rather than the South Vietnamese, who appeared to be winning the battle for the hearts and minds of the Vietnamese people. The war claimed a massive cost in young lives (some 58,000 Americans died in Vietnam) and hurt U.S. prestige around the world. Atrocities such as the March 1968 My Lai massacre committed by U.S. G.I.s also helped turn the nation against the war. Eventually, the conflict drove President Johnson from office and wounded Americans' pride and confidence for years into the future.

On this page, clockwise from top left, are scenes from a war that seemed endless: U.S. troops throw hand grenades in 1969; a tough American soldier strikes a pose in 1971; U.S. jets drop napalm in the early 1960s; wounded G.I.s huddle aboard a helicopter in 1965.

213

LARRY BURROWS·TIME LIFE PICTURES

Agony in Southeast Asia

This epic 1966 picture by LIFE photographer
Larry Burrows captures the full horror of
America's lengthy engagement in Vietnam.
The plight of these wounded soldiers bogged
down atop a faraway hilltop reflects the
nation's evolving view of the conflict: as a
quagmire into which young Americans were
being sent to die, in which the elusive promise
of victory did not merit the sacrifice it demanded.
The war divided the nation into two camps that
despised each other and put an end to Americans' long-cherished sense of invincibility.
When communist troops overran South
Vietnam in the spring of 1975, it marked the
first time in U.S. history that Americans had
been on the losing side of a major conflict.

Long Strange Trip

Freedom Riders in Alabama • 1961

One hundred years after the Civil War, many supposedly public facilities in the South were still racially segregated under Jim Crow laws. To open them up, large racially mixed groups boarded buses headed for Southern states and demanded to use public restrooms, water fountains and cafeterias in each town along the way. Though protected by federal laws regulating interstate transportation, these Freedom Riders were subject to relentless, violent harassment by local police and angry mobs. Above, federal troops guard a bus filled with protesters heading for Montgomery, Ala., in 1961.

214

Voting Rights March in Alabama • 1965

The struggle by African Americans to gain full equality with the nation's white majority rolled into the 1960s with strong momentum. Buoyed by the success of the 1955 Montgomery bus strike and the 1957 federal intervention in the Little Rock, Ark., schools and by President Kennedy's pledge of support, blacks and their white colleagues now took the offensive in the struggle, challenging Jim Crow laws even in the heart of the South. In 1965, protesters organized a march to bring national attention to the fact that African Americans couldn't vote in most of the South. The trek began in Selma, Ala., and was meant to end in the city of Montgomery, 50 miles distant. But it ended in violence, when white police viciously beat and gassed participants. A second march was ordered stopped by a local court. The third, right, protected by federal troops, reached Montgomery—and the world, through TV and newspaper coverage.

Mississippi Sit-In • 1962

Freedom Riders who stepped off buses in the South and attempted to integrate dime-store lunch counters like this one in Jackson, Miss., were often abused. Sit-ins like the 1962 protest above helped shame national chains into integrating Southern stores. The Civil Rights Act of 1964, guided through Congress by L.B.J., finally put an end to segregation in public facilities—and ugly scenes like this one.

March on Washington • 1963

A high point in the civil rights movement was the massive August 1963 protest at the Lincoln Memorial in the nation's capital, when more than 200,000 people were moved by the soaring rhetoric of Martin Luther King Jr.'s "I Have a Dream" speech and listened to songs by Bob Dylan, Marian Anderson and Joan Baez.

The event left many of those sympathetic to the civil rights struggle hoping that momentous social changes could be accomplished without violence and confrontation, but within two years the nation's cities would be set aflame by rioting in black neighborhoods.

122

JOHN OLSON·TIME LIFE PICTURES

LEFT: BARON WOLMAN·RETNA; RIGHT: BILL EPPRIDGE·TIME LIFE PICTURES

Turn On, Tune In, Drop Out: Enter the Hippies

If youth culture arrived in the 1950s in America, it exploded in the '60s: the term counterculture was coined to describe the free-wheeling new social mores. The rebels without a cause of the '50s had now found several: the "hippies" grew their hair long, opposed the War in Vietnam, practiced free love and dropped out of "straight" society to live as bohemians, like the family of Radcliffe College graduate Nancy Bray, above.

The era, like the equally giddy 1920s, was fueled by forbidden fruit: not alcohol, but marijuana and the new psychedelic drug LSD. At right, the band Santana performs at the 1969 Woodstock Festival in upstate New York, a high point of the hippies' heyday.

Rock, the Soundtrack of the '60s

The 1960s saw an efflorescence of popular music, driven by two key influences. Britain's Beatles thrilled kids with their upbeat, polished updates of 1950s U.S. rock 'n' roll, while Bob Dylan, the icon of the early-'60s folk-song movement, shocked his earnest fans by embracing the power of electric rock. Above, Dylan gives his first rock performance in 1965. Meanwhile, white musicians like Janis Joplin, below left, explored black blues. The Beatles' sonic ingenuity, Dylan's stinging lyrics and electric blues turned rock into the compelling clarion call of the decade's youth culture.

Pop Goes the Easel

Like music, the world of fine art was rocked by galvanic new energies in the '60s. Artists like Andy Warhol and Roy Lichtenstein baffled many when they adapted the visual language of advertising and lowbrow culture into their work. But there was a point: in Warhol's painted soup cans and Lichtenstein's comic-strip rip-offs, above, Pop Art nailed the nose-thumbing spirit of the times, even as it addressed the growing influence of mass media and marketing on American society.

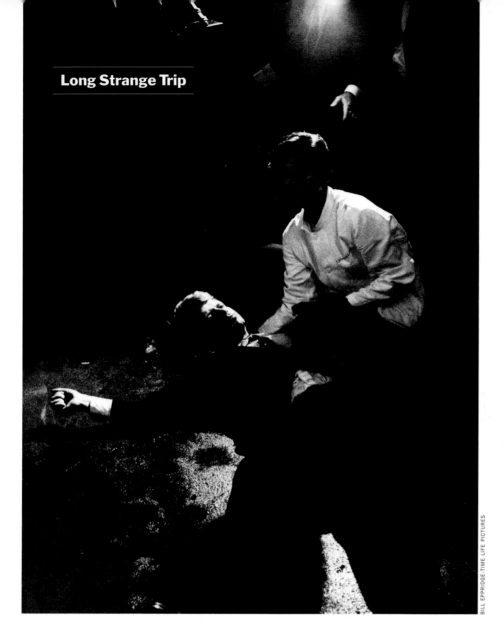

BILL EPPRIDGE-TIME LIFE PICTURES

Murder in Memphis

There was no lack of heroes in the civil rights movement of the 1950s and '60s, but its undisputed leader and the most eloquent spokesman for the hopes and dreams of African Americans was the Rev. Martin Luther King Jr. It was King who led the bus boycott in Montgomery, Ala., and who electrified those marching on Washington in 1963 with his historic address, "I Have a Dream." After a white assassin, James Earl Ray, gunned down King at a Memphis motel on April 4, 1968, right, blacks rioted in many big-city ghettos.

Great Lives Cut Short by Assassins' Bullets • 1968

By the late 1960s, the U.S. was a deeply divided nation: the War in Vietnam, the fault lines caused by the youthful counterculture and battles over race and segregation pitted American against American perhaps more deeply than at any time since the Civil War. The mix was already volatile, but when assassins struck down two of America's most prominent voices for healing and unity, New York Senator Robert Kennedy and civil rights leader Martin Luther King Jr., a sickening sense that the nation was running off the rails became pervasive.

Senator Kennedy, brother of the slain President, announced he would run for the White House shortly before Lyndon Johnson declared he would not run, in March 1968. Kennedy appeared to be a good bet to win the Democratic nomination when he was shot and killed, left, by Sirhan Sirhan, a Palestinian immigrant to the U.S., on June 5, 1968, only two months after King was killed.

JOSEPH LOUW-TIME LIFE PICTURES-GETTY IMAGES

PERRY C. RIDDLE—CHICAGO DAILY NEWS

Meltdown in Chicago • 1968

America's lengthy War in Vietnam spawned the widest popular protests against government policy of the 20th century. Originally such marches were generally peaceful, but as tensions over the war heated up and the anger between hawks and doves mounted, the mostly youthful protesters began engaging in more and more acts of civil disobedience. Lines were drawn: all cops were "pigs" and all the youngsters were traitors. In one of the largest protests, some 200,000 demonstrators marched on the Pentagon on Oct. 21, 1967, to protest U.S. policy. The following summer angry protesters filled the streets of Chicago at the Democratic National Convention, left, and the city's police responded with vicious assaults that a federal commission of inquiry later described as "a police riot."

Dark Side of the Age of Aquarius • 1969

Mid-1960s hippies, who trafficked in a philosophy long on love, mysticism and "flower power," initially were seen as charming, colorful innocents. But the ease with which that innocence could be diverted to evil ends was brought home forcefully by the bloody, senseless string of multiple murders conducted by the outlaw hippie cult led by Charles Manson, left, in Los Angeles in 1969.

Simmering Cities Ignite with Racial Violence

As America's lengthy era of racial segregation finally ended and the battle for black civil rights continued, tensions long suppressed erupted in cities around the country. Rioting on a large scale broke out in the Watts ghetto in Los Angeles in August 1965; soon other cities were in flames. Below a National Guardsman stands watch in Detroit in 1967; above, a riot scene in Newark, N.J., one month earlier.

The riots, essentially an outcry of despair, angered and frightened many whites and divided cities further along racial lines. Historians are still arguing over whether the riots hampered or accelerated efforts to achieve full equality for the nation's African Americans.

219

Rocket Men

The Soviets jump-started the space race with the launch of Sputnik in 1957; John F. Kennedy kicked it into overdrive with his 1961 challenge to Americans to land a man on the moon by the end of the 1960s. The contest with the Soviets was part science, part cold war posturing, part marketing, part pure exploration—and a fully exhilarating ride for rocket jocks and spectators alike. Along the way, the original seven Mercury program astronauts (right, in 1959) were lionized, and John Glenn, below, became a hero when he made the first U.S. orbital flight of Earth in 1962.

Gemini Program Gloves
In the 10 manned Gemini missions (1965-66), NASA developed the tools it later used to land men on the moon.

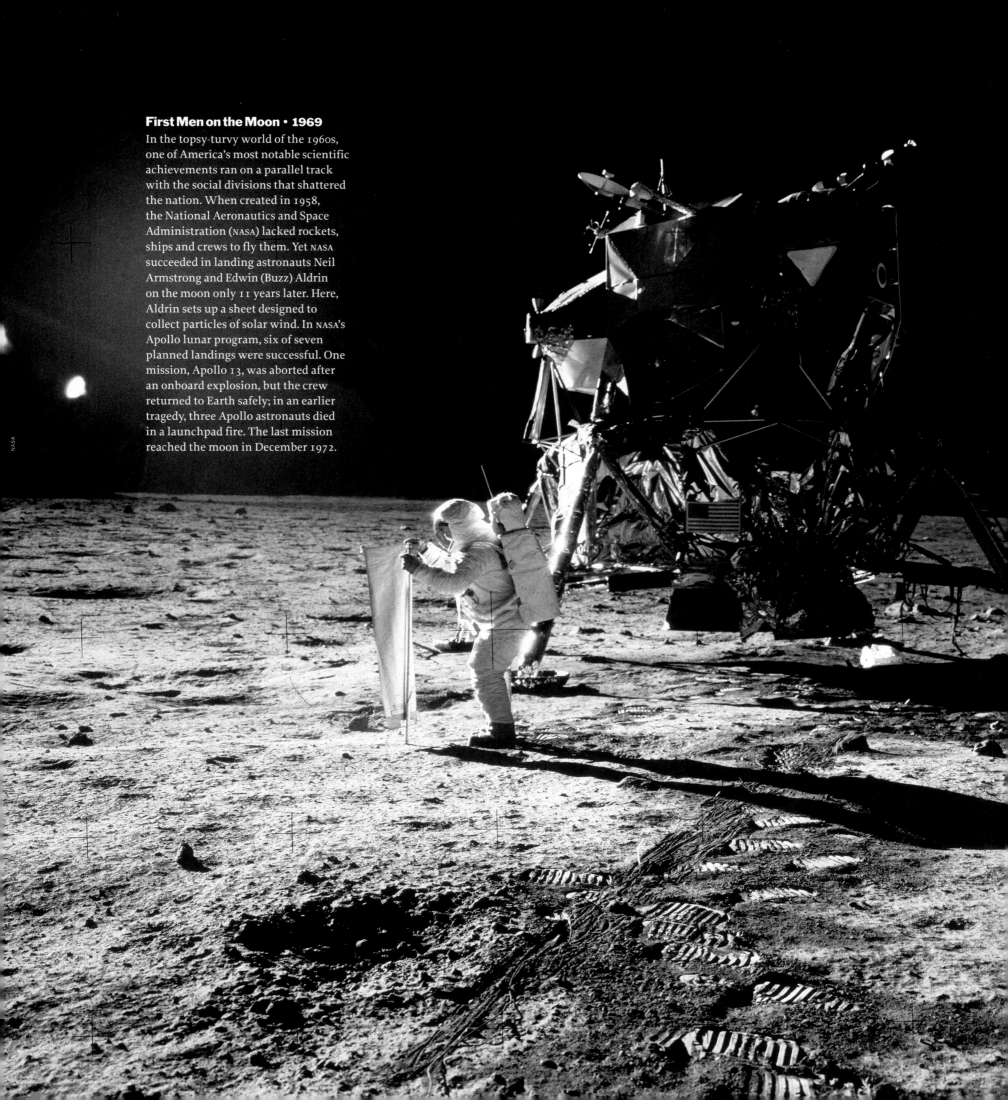

First Men on the Moon · 1969

In the topsy-turvy world of the 1960s, one of America's most notable scientific achievements ran on a parallel track with the social divisions that shattered the nation. When created in 1958, the National Aeronautics and Space Administration (NASA) lacked rockets, ships and crews to fly them. Yet NASA succeeded in landing astronauts Neil Armstrong and Edwin (Buzz) Aldrin on the moon only 11 years later. Here, Aldrin sets up a sheet designed to collect particles of solar wind. In NASA's Apollo lunar program, six of seven planned landings were successful. One mission, Apollo 13, was aborted after an onboard explosion, but the crew returned to Earth safely; in an earlier tragedy, three Apollo astronauts died in a launchpad fire. The last mission reached the moon in December 1972.

1970-80

Out of Gas

TWO HELICOPTER FLIGHTS, SEPARATED IN TIME BY ONLY EIGHT MONTHS, SUM UP THE AMERICA OF the 1970s. The first, above, was taken on Aug. 9, 1974, by Richard Nixon, who became the only President to resign his office, following the long Watergate crisis, in which his White House was found to have engaged in criminal activities for political ends. The second flight was taken by Americans fleeing from a lost war. The nation's long commitment to South Vietnam ended in full, humiliating retreat in April 1975, as North Vietnamese troops rolled into the nation's capital city, Saigon, and the last Americans at the U.S. embassy scrambled to the rooftop to escape by chopper.

In this most dismal era since the 1930s, the limitations of U.S. power suddenly became apparent, when the nation's reliance on imported energy sparked a pair of oil shortages that rocked the economy. At home, Americans were increasingly divided by the conflicts over cultural standards that began in the 1960s. Fittingly, the decade ended with a whimper, with 52 Americans being held hostage in Tehran, Iran's capital, by revolutionaries who had toppled the nation's pro-U.S. government.

"You see paralysis and stagnation and drift.
You don't like it, and neither do I. What can we do?"

—JIMMY CARTER, JULY 15, 1979

A President's Historic Journey Opens Doorways to a Longtime Communist Foe • 1972

Whatever his failings, Richard Nixon was a statesman with rare strategic vision: he stunned the world when he declared he would visit Asia's enigmatic communist giant, China, in February 1972. In a single deft stroke, Nixon paved the way for diplomatic relations with the planet's most populous nation, which had been officially ignored for decades by Washington, and overturned a generation's worth of conventional wisdom about the supposedly monolithic communist world. That the diplomatic volte-face was launched by perhaps the most ostentatiously anticommunist politician of the cold war era only added to its drama. Toward the end of his life, Nixon reflected, "I will be known historically for two things: Watergate and the opening to China."

White House "Dirty Tricks" Force a Presidential Resignation • 1974

After White House staffers and former CIA employees were arrested breaking into the headquarters of the Democratic National Committee in the capital's Watergate complex in the summer of 1972, Richard Nixon's White House accurately characterized the event as a "third-rate burglary attempt." No one imagined that the amateurish break-in could bring down a President as popular and powerful as Nixon. But two junior crime reporters at the Washington *Post*, Carl Bernstein and Bob Woodward, left, traced the operation's trail straight to the Oval Office. In less than a year, congressional investigators had implicated several key Nixon aides in covering up White House involvement, while a Senate committee led by North Carolina Senator Sam Ervin, center, uncovered audiotapes that showed Nixon was involved in the cover-up. In August 1974, rather than face near certain impeachment, Nixon became the first President to resign. He was succeeded by his recently appointed Vice President, Gerald Ford, right, who gave Nixon a full pardon. Ford was widely criticized at the time, but at his death in 2006 he was hailed for having put an end to the affair.

In Saigon, April Becomes the Cruelest Month • 1975

After taking office in August 1974 as the nation's first unelected President, Gerald Ford was faced with the final unraveling of America's long involvement in Vietnam. By the spring of 1975, the U.S. client regime in South Vietnam was beyond saving and North Vietnamese forces were circling the capital. On the last day of April, the U.S. radio station in Saigon began playing *White Christmas* over and over again: it was the signal for Americans to report to evacuation points. In a heroic airlift that involved hundreds of helicopter sorties and flights aboard packed cargo planes, some 6,000 Americans and more than 50,000 South Vietnamese allies escaped the country. While North Vietnamese tanks smashed through the gates of South Vietnam's presidential palace, above, thousands of South Vietnamese clamored and fought to enter the U.S. embassy and board the last helicopters lifting off from its roof. Amid the debacle, there was no denying the truth: America had lost the war.

225

An America Short on Confidence Runs Short on Energy

A nation whose powers seemed almost endless after its great two-front victory in World War II finally bumped up against its limits in the 1970s, in the form of shortages of the magic elixir that had fueled the postwar tide of national prosperity: cheap gasoline. Americans' romance with their "wheels" involved a strong dose of denial, for the petroleum that drove the nation's growth was increasingly not produced at home. Reality set in after two 1970s petroleum crises sparked panic and long lines at gas stations like the Chicago business above in 1974.

The first energy scare came in 1973, when the price of oil doubled after the Organization of Arab Petroleum Exporting Countries (OAPEC) stopped shipping oil to America, in retaliation for U.S. support of Israel in that year's October War. In 1979 Iran stopped exporting oil after its revolution, forcing prices up; President Jimmy Carter donned a cardigan and lowered the White House thermostat to encourage his constituents to conserve energy. But when gas prices fell sharply within a few years, Americans put the pedal to the metal again. The nation's energy problems seemed to vanish in the rearview mirror—although they were much larger than they appeared to be.

Dawn of Environmental Awareness • 1970

Concerns for the state of Planet Earth and its environment began as a trickle, with the 1962 publication of Rachel Carson's best seller *Silent Spring.* The sense of the planet as a single organism was reinforced by the revelatory photographs of the era—like the 1972 image below, taken from a NASA lunar orbiter, which allowed humans to see their planet as a whole for the first time in history. Decrying the rising tide of damage inflicted on the environment by man, scientists and concerned citizens, led by U.S. Senator Gaylord Nelson, gathered on the first Earth Day in 1970 to call for a new appreciation of a planet in peril. At left, "greens" rally in New York City on that day.

A Ruling on Abortion Heats Up America's "Culture Wars" • 1973

On Jan. 22, 1973, the U.S. Supreme Court ruled to legalize abortion in the case of *Roe v. Wade*. Over time, that controversial decision would create the single most compelling and divisive social issue in American life since the nation split into two camps over the ethics of slavery and abolition in the 19th century. Social conservatives and religious leaders, who considered abortion a form of murder, denounced the ruling and would spend decades working diligently to overturn it, although a 2007 CNN poll showed that 62% of Americans support a woman's right to an abortion. In 1983, 10 years after *Roe*, some 1.6 million abortions were performed in the U.S.; by 2007 a much smaller percentage of pregnant women underwent the procedure. Yet the division of the nation into "pro-life" and "pro-choice" positions continues to shape U.S. political life.

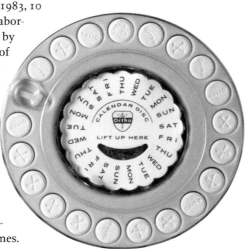

The contraceptive pill, right, first widely used in the 1960s and '70s, removed one of the oldest social barriers to sexual activity, the fear of an unwanted pregnancy, and helped fuel the so-called sexual revolution of the times.

Once Again, Protests for Women's Rights

The questioning of American social structures that began in the 1960s led to lasting changes in the lives of U.S. women, as feminist groups like the National Organization for Women helped lead a gender revolution in the '70s. The "women's liberation" movement enouraged more women to attend college, enter the workforce and demand equality with men in every area of life, from the home to the workplace.

Amid Vast Social Change, a Cry from the Right • 1979

The deep divisions that marked American life in the 1960s only grew wider in the 1970s, as families and neighbors argued about Richard Nixon, the War in Vietnam, abortion, women's liberation and the nation's ongoing re-examination of longstanding social norms, which was either overdue or outrageous, depending upon one's views. Religious and social conservatives denounced values they saw as deeply antithetical to their beliefs and began to unite to oppose them.

In 1979 Virginia's Rev. Jerry Falwell founded the Moral Majority, an interest group devoted to bringing a more outspoken Fundamentalist Christian perspective to U.S. political life. Decades later, at Falwell's death in May 2007, the so-called culture wars still divided the U.S.

229

MAKIN' WHOOPEE: THE SEXUAL REVOLUTION

Sex was long a taboo topic in Calvinist America, but some in the '70s had a different idea: "If it feels good, do it"

When Skin Was In

At a time of widespread disillusionment with politics and international affairs, many Americans chose to focus on personal concerns, inspiring journalist Tom Wolfe to coin the enduring tag for the era: the "Me decade." The argument went, if you can't change the world, you can at least change your consciousness—like the folks at left, shedding clothes and hang-ups at the Esalen Institute in Big Sur, Calif., which was a seaside hothouse for many of the era's myriad self-help therapies.

One result of the movement, aided by the questioning of social taboos in the 1960s, was a striking new interest and frankness about sexuality in mainstream culture: best-seller lists filled up with how-to books, above; actors bared all on Broadway in *Oh! Calcutta!;* "skin" magazines like *Penthouse* prospered; and the New York *Times* shocked some readers when it reviewed the hard-core porn film *Deep Throat*.

Disco Gets Americans Spinning Again

By the 1970s, rock was awash in bombast and had lost its roll—until the simple, propulsive beats of disco music, as embodied by a magnetic John Travolta in the 1977 film *Saturday Night Fever*, got Americans polishing up their dancing shoes.

High Tide for Big-Screen Rebels

Music was the preferred vehicle for passion and protest in the 1960s, but in the 1970s the movies caught up, as a new batch of maverick young directors began creating highly individual films that, in retrospect, are seen as a golden age of creativity in Hollywood. Robert Altman, John Sayles and Martin Scorsese led the movement; Robert De Niro, left, starred in Scorsese's tough 1976 dissection of urban despair, *Taxi Driver*.

When Darkness Dazzled

Reflecting the nation's mood, arts and culture turned sour in the 1970s, as the idyllic, failed dreams of the 1960s came to seem almost comical in their innocence. Hippies, sunshine and pot were out; glitzy revelers who crowded New York City's flashiest disco, Studio 54, right, snorted cocaine and took downer drugs like Quaaludes.

Scenemakers of a decadent decade included, from left, artist Andy Warhol, model Jerry Hall, singer Debbie Harry of pop group Blondie and writer Truman Capote, in hat.

"Live from New York, It's Saturday Night!"

Before the advent of cable television in the late 1970s, TV programming was firmly controlled by three major broadcast networks, which favored cautious, mainstream fare. Although shows like *All in the Family* pushed the bland limits of the form, it was the Oct. 11, 1975, debut of NBC's *Saturday Night Live* that brought the voice of the youthful counterculture into the nation's living rooms. Above, the initial cast polishes its attitude.

TONY TRIOLO—SPORTS ILLUSTRATED

NO CREDIT

A Champion Returns to Form

As a draft-resisting Black Muslim, Muhammad Ali was reviled by many in the 1960s for his political views, but he won the respect of fans again with such legendary fights as his 1974 "Rumble in the Jungle" with George Foreman in Zaïre, above. Ali became one of the most beloved Americans on the planet and an international icon of courage and athletics.

Music Gets Punked

Stripping rock of its 1960s pretensions and prettiness, New York City band the Ramones returned the music to its ragged three-chord roots in songs that celebrated primitive skills and pleasures. The sound soon found its perfect name: punk rock.

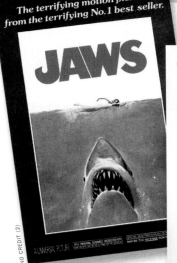

NO CREDIT (2)

Inventing the Blockbuster

Even as Hollywood embraced quirky art films in the '70s, directors Steven Spielberg and George Lucas pointed the way to a future of blockbusters with two landmark hits, *Jaws* (1975) and *Star Wars* (1977).

A Revolution Spawns a Hostage Crisis • 1979

For decades Iran was a staunch U.S. ally in the turbulent Middle East, until exiled religious leader Ayatullah Ruhollah Khomeini sparked a fundamentalist Islamic revolution in 1979. Later that year, President Jimmy Carter admitted the deposed, terminally ill Shah of Iran to the U.S. for medical treatment. Shortly afterward, on Nov. 5, a group of radical students over-ran the U.S. embassy in Tehran and took 70 Americans hostage. Khomeini refused to release 52 of them—for days, then weeks, then months. In April 1980, a high-risk rescue plan failed miserably, as U.S. helicopters crashed and burned in the Iranian desert. Khomeini finally freed his captives in 1981, 444 days after they were taken prisoner, but in a final slap at Carter, the Iranian mullah delayed their release until after Ronald Reagan became President.

The U.S. Brokers a Breakthrough Peace Plan • 1978

Americans savored a diplomatic triumph in September 1978: after 12 days of secret talks led by President Carter at the Camp David presidential retreat, Egyptian President Anwar Sadat, left, and Israeli Prime Minister Menachem Begin agreed on a framework for peace for their nations, at war since 1948. Almost 30 years later, this historic first treaty between the Jewish state and one of its Arab neighbors remains the single greatest U.S. success in decades of attempts to bring stability to a strife-torn region. How much work remained to be done was underscored three years later, when Sadat was assassinated by Islamic militants within his own country. Below left, the formal signing ceremony was held at the White House on Sept. 17.

233

1980-88

Masters of
The Universe

234

THE STORY OF AMERICA HAS A RHYTHM AND SWAY OF ITS OWN, AS PERIODS OF unrest and challenge alternate with eras of comfort and prosperity. So it is with the 1980s, which, apart from the inevitable evolutions of styles, slang and status symbols, might easily be mistaken for the 1950s—or, for that matter, the 1880s. After decades of social upheaval, Americans weary of turmoil and debate seemed to call a truce and trade in their swords—not for plowshares but for shares—shares in prosperous new corporations; shares in an updated, aggressively materialistic American Dream; shares in the new 401(k) retirement plans that became a symbol of '80s security. Some Americans were left behind in the boom, and the slickness and greed of such era-defining figures as New York City developer Donald Trump were excessive, but for many women and blacks the 1980s brought a chance to share in the opportunities long enjoyed by others.

As in the 1950s, a beloved father figure, Ronald Reagan, presided over this era of avaricious Wall Streeters, suburban "McMansions" and personal computers. Writer Tom Wolfe, who termed the 1970s the "Me decade," called the nation's power-suited young strivers "Masters of the Universe." Indeed, with the Soviet Union in decline and a fresh surge of patriotism painting the decade red, white and blue, the nation's future in the 1980s seemed limitless, as glittering and ascendant as a Trump Tower escalator.

" 'Cause the boy with the cold hard cash
Is always Mister Right, cause we are
Living in a material world
And I am a material girl."

—*MATERIAL GIRL*, PETER BROWN AND ROBERT RANS,
RECORDED BY MADONNA, 1985

A Sunny-Side-Up Presidency Begins with a Flourish • 1981

Ronald Reagan was widely admired during his time in office, and his reputation among ordinary citizens, if not historians, has only grown with the passing years: a 2007 Gallup poll ranked the "Great Communicator" second only to Abraham Lincoln as the greatest U.S. President in the minds of Americans. The former Hollywood actor's long run of good fortune and success began on Jan. 20, 1981, when Iran released the U.S. hostages it had held for 444 days at the exact moment Reagan was being sworn in—a gesture of defiance by Iran's ruler, Ayatullah Ruhollah Khomeini, against Jimmy Carter.

Reagan earned Americans' respect with his courage in the face of an early assassination attempt, his sunny optimism and his firm political beliefs, but his record includes both failures and triumphs. He helped restore America's pride, badly wounded in the 1960s and '70s by the setbacks of Vietnam and Watergate. His covert support for Islamic guerrillas fighting Soviet invaders in Afghanistan helped hasten the end of a Soviet regime he once famously described as "an evil empire," but his last years in office were marked by the revelation of his White House's illegal Iran-*contra* scheme. Sadly, only a few latter-day Republicans and Democrats have embraced a quality that set Reagan apart among American politicians in the last decades of the 20th century: his refusal to demonize his political enemies.

THE REAGAN ERA

Ronald Reagan was the first President to serve two full terms in office since Dwight D. Eisenhower in the 1950s. Reagan's years in office saw the final duels of the cold war, as he challenged the Soviets in Central America and Afghanistan and with a massive arms build-up

1981: A Close Call in Washington

Just 10 weeks after taking office, Reagan was shot by John Hinckley Jr., a mentally deranged young man. Although the President was seriously wounded, his famous wit was unimpaired. He told wife Nancy, "Honey, I forgot to duck."

1983: Islamic Terrorists Strike in Beirut

On Oct. 23 suicide bombers from Lebanon's radical Hizballah faction killed 241 U.S. troops, right, sent to Lebanon by Reagan to keep the peace in a brutal civil war.

Mid-1980s: Proxy Wars In the Americas

The Reagan Doctrine declared the U.S. would firmly oppose communist regimes; his Administration applied it with zeal in Central America, where the U.S. funneled arms to rightist rebel groups in the region in hopes of subverting Nicaragua's pro-Moscow Sandinista regime, above.

1986: Arms and the Man

Lieut. Colonel Oliver North, left, ran a secret operation that sold weapons to anti-U.S. Iran and sent the profits to Central American rightists. Exposure of the plan rocked the nation.

1988: Twilight of the Cold War

Reagan's hard line against the U.S.S.R. softened after new leader Mikhail Gorbachev began trying to reform the Soviet system. Reagan, formerly a critic of arms-control talks, visited Moscow's Red Square in 1988, where he signed a treaty to reduce U.S. and Soviet nuclear weapons.

A Space Shuttle Calamity • 1986

On the morning of Jan. 28, 1986, millions of American schoolkids trained their eyes on classroom TV sets as the space shuttle *Challenger* blasted off on a six-day mission. Interest in the launch was especially high because NASA had included New Hampshire schoolteacher Christa McAuliffe on the mission, in an attempt to reignite the interest in space exploration that the agency had achieved in the 1960s.

But only 73 seconds after liftoff, the craft blew apart, leaving the ghastly signature of failure at right, forever burned into the memories of Americans alive at the time. All seven astronauts aboard were killed. A commission of inquiry later determined that the explosion was caused by the freezing of a small rubber ring in a rocket booster and that NASA officials had failed to address warnings from engineers of just such an event if the craft was launched on a cold day.

From Tragedy to Triumph • 1990

Four short years after the deadly explosion that killed the *Challenger* astronauts, NASA scored one of its greatest achievements with the April 24, 1990, launch of the orbiting Hubble Space Telescope, named for influential U.S. astronomer Edwin Hubble.

The images sent back to Earth by Hubble's high-powered array of cameras and sensors—like this picture of giant clouds of gas in the Eagle Nebula some 7,000 light-years away—gave humans new reasons to marvel at the grandeur of the heavens. But the Hubble had its problems as well: the main reflecting mirror of the telescope was ground improperly. It was successfully patched up by a repair mission in December 1993. In need of further repairs as of early 2007, the Hubble is due for another rescue mission, currently scheduled for September 2008. The black area at the top right of this picture is a region not photographed by the telescope.

A Pandemic's Toll, Stitched into Cloth and Memory

The original, unofficial name of the disease was as grim as it was imprecise: "gay cancer." When doctors discovered in the early 1980s that large numbers of homosexual men in New York City, Los Angeles and San Francisco were suddenly developing a previously rare form of cancer, Kaposi's sarcoma, fact blended with speculation to create nightmares for a community already ostracized by mainstream society. In truth, the cancer proved to be only one product of a new syndrome that made the victim vulnerable to numerous diseases by disabling the body's immune system. Renamed AIDS (for acquired immunodeficiency syndrome) in 1982, the illness ravaged one community after another: intravenous drug users, recipients of tainted blood transfusions, Haitians, pregnant woman and their newborns, Africans and more. Sadly, both the Reagan Administration and U.S. society were slow to address the ravages of the blood-borne disease; the AIDS Quilt below, begun in 1985 by activist Cleve Jones, with patches that celebrate the lives of some 91,000 victims of AIDS, finally helped communicate the disease's toll.

Twenty-five years into the AIDS era, new drug therapies have proved effective in slowing the progress of the syndrome within individual patients—for those who can afford them—while education has helped impede its spread. The bad news: by 2007, more than 500,000 Americans and some 25 million people worldwide are believed to have died from what is now a global pandemic for which a cure has yet to be found.

The Computer Gets Personal

Thanks to a technological breakthrough of the late 1940s, the tiny transistor, and a second breakthrough in 1959, the integrated circuit, electronic computers that once occupied entire rooms began moving into America's living rooms in the early 1980s. A pair of battling computer geeks led the charge: Bill Gates, shown at left with his early partner at Microsoft, Paul Allen, made IBM's first personal computers possible with a crucial piece of organizing software, the Disk Operating System. The Apple machines of Steve Jobs, below, offered a snazzy point-and-click graphic interface that was both fun and functional; Apple depicted IBM as "Big Brother" in the 1984 commercial above. Market leader Microsoft went on to create Windows, a lookalike of the Apple desktop— and the two companies have battled it out for digital dominance ever since.

Pop Music Gets Slick and Rap Beats Get Thick

On Aug. 1, 1981, a new cable-TV channel, MTV (Music Television), began broadcasting, playing a song by the British group the Buggles titled *Video Killed the Radio Star.* The advent of MTV didn't kill radio, but it altered the pop-music landscape, breeding elaborate video versions of songs, the most famous of which was the ghoulish *Thriller,* above right, by the gifted showman and dancer Michael Jackson. Video also supercharged the career of the sexy "Material Girl," Madonna, and helped turn the poetic New Jersey populist Bruce Springsteen into a stadium-filling, anthem-singing icon. Meanwhile, African Americans began rocking the nation with an entirely new sound, rap. As practiced by pioneers like Run-D.M.C., rap featured a rhythm track stripped to basic beats, with clever lyrics spoken and chanted above it.

Athletes Soar into History

Propelled by a strong economy and professional marketing tactics, sports became far more corporate in the money-mad 1980s. Although stars now began earning enormous salaries, no one doubted that such athletes as Wayne Gretzky, Magic Johnson and Larry Bird deserved their wealth.

In basketball, even other players were awed by the Chicago Bulls' Michael Jordan, left, whose flashy dunks and all-around court artistry left fans breathless. The greatest game of the era came at the 1980 Winter Olympics at Lake Placid, N.Y., right, when the U.S. hockey squad beat a strong team from the U.S.S.R.

Los Angeles' Golden Games

In a sports-crazed era, when the rallying cry "Go for It!" became America's unofficial slogan, the 1984 Olympic Games in Los Angeles were a star-spangled mash-up of patriotism, market-ing, spectacle and, lest we forget, exciting athletics.

U.S. star sprinter and long-jumper Carl Lewis, right, took home four gold medals, while ebullient Mary Lou Retton, above, vaulted to a gold medal and the cover of Wheaties boxes with her dazzling gymnastic routines.

"Until now, the world we've known has been a world divided—
a world of barbed wire and concrete block, conflict and cold
war. Now, we can see a new world coming into view."

—GEORGE H.W. BUSH, "NEW WORLD ORDER" SPEECH, MARCH 6, 1991

245

1989-1999
New World Order

NOT EVERY BATTLE ENDS WITH THE U.S. MARINES RAISING THE STARS AND STRIPES OVER ENEMY territory. The cold war, America's long, bitter duel with Soviet communism, ended in 1989 not with the sound of bugles blowing but with the crunch of the sledgehammers that brought down the Berlin Wall, the hated symbol of the divisions between East and West Germany, communism and capitalism, the U.S.S.R. and the U.S. There are many reasons America triumphed in its long duel with the Soviet Union, and not all of them involved politics, arms or diplomacy: as amply documented in this volume, Western society offered freedom of speech and worship, the opportunity for personal growth and the lure of riches, as well as freedom of expression in the arts, which helped create an exuberant national cultural life that was always lively and buoyant, if sometimes tawdry. In a sign of the world's new political order, less than two years after the Wall fell, President George H.W. Bush rallied a broad-based coalition that rolled back Iraqi strongman Saddam Hussein's power grab in Kuwait. Enlisting as allies such odd bed-fellows as Russia, Israel, Syria and Japan, the President did not seem to be overreaching when he declared that in the wake of the cold war, a "new world order" was being born.

247

Operation Desert Storm Liberates Kuwait • 1991

Emboldened by the fall of the Berlin Wall—and bucked up
by a gritty ally, Britain's Prime Minister Margaret Thatcher—
President George H.W. Bush acted quickly and decisively in
August 1990 after Iraqi dictator Saddam Hussein sent tanks
and troops rolling into Kuwait, his oil-rich neighbor to the
south, in a blatant grab for petroleum and power. Bush
denounced the deed, enlisted the support of a wide-ranging
and surprising group of allies—including Russia, Japan, Syria,
Israel, Saudi Arabia and others—and then took the case for
confronting Saddam to an approving United Nations and
the U.S. Congress.

The skies over Baghdad lit up with antiaircraft fire on the
night of Jan. 17, 1991, as U.S. and British aircraft launched the
first war the world watched unfolding in real time. Five weeks
later, coalition troops charged into Iraq and Kuwait from
Saudi Arabia, overwhelming Saddam's poorly armed, poorly
disciplined armies. On Feb. 27, Kuwait City, the capital, was
liberated; at left, U.S. troops march in Kuwait after the victory,
where a defeated Saddam had set the oil fields ablaze. The
well-executed strategy of Operation Desert Storm won the
renewed respect of their countrymen for the U.S. armed forces:
above, the President visits U.S. soldiers in Saudi Arabia in
December 1990, weeks before the invasion. Citing fears
of unleashing a civil war that would pin U.S. troops in an
occupied, divided nation, Bush left Saddam in power, a
decision that was widely criticized at the time. Yet from
the perspective of 2007, Bush's fears seem prescient.

A White House Sex Scandal Mars a Presidency • 1998-99

In a political era marked by deep partisan divisions, President Bill Clinton was a lightning rod for criticism. When a long inquiry into a decade-old real estate deal went nowhere, it morphed, almost overnight, into questions of whether Clinton had been sexually involved with Monica Lewinsky, a White House intern, above, and had lied to the nation about it. After much evasion and delay, he was proved to have done so. The G.O.P.-led House impeached Clinton; the Senate, following a verdict reached earlier in the court of public opinion, acquitted him. "Monicagate" cast a self-induced shadow over the last two years of Clinton's presidency.

"Not Guilty" • 1995

Exposing lingering racial divides in American life, whites recoiled even as many blacks rejoiced on Oct. 3, 1995, when, after a highly publicized trial, retired pro football star O.J. Simpson was found not guilty of the brutal 1994 murders of his wife Nicole and her friend Ronald Goldman.

Simpson was found liable for the two deaths in a civil trial three years later and was ordered to pay a settlement of $33.5 million.

Home-Grown Terror Strikes in the Heartland • 1995

The long-simmering antigovernment sentiments of the nation's far-right groups boiled over into violence in the 1990s. The movement had seemed harmless, if outspoken and paranoid, until a U.S. Army veteran decorated in Operation Desert Storm, Timothy McVeigh, pulled up to Oklahoma City's Alfred P. Murrah Federal Building on April 19, 1995, and lit two fuses to the 7,000-lb. fertilizer bomb in his rental truck. The explosion vaporized the front of the building, killing 168 people, including 19 children. Tried and convicted, McVeigh claimed until his 2001 execution that his deed was the act of a heroic patriot rather than a terrorist.

249

The World Wide Web Boots Up

The spectacular rise of the computer is one of the great sagas of modern technology. In the 1990s the dazzling machines began to alter society in revolutionary ways, thanks to the World Wide Web, a communications interface invented by Briton Tim Berners-Lee and given graphic life by a team of Americans led by Marc Andreessen. The breakthrough connected all the machines in a new digital realm, the Internet, above; by the decade's end, e-mail and Web-based companies like America Online, Amazon and eBay had transformed commerce and communication.

In Sports, Two for the Ages

No one could have predicted that Americans would flip for the European-dominated sport of bicycle racing, but when Texas-born Lance Armstrong, below, beat a bout of testicular cancer and then won the sport's premier event, the Tour de France, in 1999, the bandwagon got rolling. Armstrong went to win the Tour six more times, entering the pantheon of U.S. sports heroes.

Joining Armstrong in glory was golfer Tiger Woods, who was widely considered the best player in history before he turned 30. Woods staked his claim to legendary status when, at 21, he dominated his first major event, the 1997 Masters championship, winning by 12 strokes.

251

From Grunge to Ghetto Fab, Music's Dread Allure

Predictable as a pendulum, pop music in the 1990s swung away from the slickness of the '80s, as "grunge" groups like the plaid-clad Seattle trio Nirvana wrote urgent, dark anthems. The group's charismatic songwriter Kurt Cobain, left, took his own life in 1994.

Rap beats dominated the decade, as the bottom-heavy music proved richly malleable, a vehicle for themes from sex and romance to protest and buffoonery. "Gangsta rap" stars like Tupac Shakur, above, celebrated "thug life," without irony: Shakur was killed in a drive-by shooting in 1996.

An Empathetic Bundle of Energy Talks Her Way to the Top

Oprah Winfrey was born in 1954 to a pair of unwed, impoverished Mississippi teens. Forty years later, she was one of the richest, most widely recognized and most powerful women in the world. While the rise of the TV talk-show host may have been unlikely, Winfrey earned her renown, sporting a way with words, an agile mind, a gift for connecting with audiences of all sorts—and the demanding drive of a diva. Her immense clout was best displayed when she began a monthly TV book club in 1996: thanks to the "Oprah effect," each title she chose became a huge best seller.

New Century, New Challenges

AMERICA SURGED INTO THE 21ST CENTURY WITH A FOLLOWING WIND: THE FUTURE SEEMED LIMITLESS FOR THE world's lone superpower, now the engine of the Internet revolution that was transforming global society. But all too soon, utopian visions butted up against reality. The first presidential election of the new century turned into a bitter stalemate, with the nation's fate hanging on bits of paper dangling from punchcard ballots. The U.S. Supreme Court declared Republican George W. Bush the winner, dividing the nation. Then, only eight months after Bush was inaugurated, a group of Islamist terrorists successfully attacked America's home soil, bringing the Twin Towers of New York City's World Trade Center crashing to the ground, shattering Americans' sense of physical isolation from the problems of the Old World and plunging the nation into a deadly new conflict with an unfamiliar, frightening enemy.

"We've never been braver. We've never been stronger."
—RUDOLPH GIULIANI, MAYOR OF NEW YORK CITY, SEPT. 17, 2001

The U.S. and Its Allies Topple the Taliban • 2001

Less than a month after the terrorist attacks of Sept. 11, 2001, President George W. Bush dispatched U.S. forces to Afghanistan, where the extremist Islamic Taliban regime had for years given shelter to Saudi-born al-Qaeda terrorist leader Osama bin Laden, perpetrator of the attack. A cataclysmic aerial bombardment followed. Within weeks, some 4,000 U.S. forces, left, joined by Western allies and anti-Taliban Afghan warlords, drove the Islamists from power. But bin Laden and his chief deputy, Egyptian Ayman al-Zawahiri, escaped and have never been captured. After their 2001 fall from power, the Taliban have regrouped: in 2007, they remained a potent guerrilla force, undermining the U.S.-sponsored regime of Afghan President Hamid Karzai.

255

Election Deadlock • 2000

When polls closed in voting for the presidency on Nov. 7, 2000, Republican George W. Bush and Democrat Al Gore were each within a hair's breadth of winning the presidency. Florida's 25 votes in the Electoral College would decide the outcome. Thus began a month-long drama, fought out in recount rooms and the courts, over such seeming minutiae as hanging chads (partially detached bits of paper from punch-hole ballots) and butterfly ballots (the design of which may have confused some voters). Above, an election monitor eyes a ballot during the recount.

On Dec. 12, the U.S. Supreme Court ordered that the Florida recount must stop, awarding Bush the state of Florida—and the presidency. Bush became only the fourth President to take office after garnering fewer popular votes than his opponent. Above, the two candidates shake hands on a snowy December day in the nation's capital and agree to move on after the verdict.

256

An Intervention in Iraq Results in a Lengthy Occupation • 2003-07

After a U.S.-led coalition deposed Afghanistan's Taliban regime, the Bush Administration escalated what it called the "war on terror," directing a steady drumbeat of accusations and threats at Iraq. Charging Saddam Hussein with building weapons of mass destruction and lending critical support to al-Qaeda, the White House received congressional authorization in October 2002 to use force to remove the Iraqi strongman. Government inquiries later showed neither of the claims used as a rationale for the invasion was correct.

The shooting war began on March 20, 2003, and was over in less than six weeks, prompting President George W. Bush to declare "the end of major combat operations in Iraq" in an exuberant May 1 speech aboard an aircraft carrier, above. Saddam was captured in December 2003 and was tried and sentenced to death in 2006. But the U.S.-led occupation was poorly managed, and a deadly insurgency flared up, fed by Islamic sectarian hatreds long kept in check by Saddam.

A U.S.-installed government successfully held elections in 2006 but lost prestige when Saddam's execution appeared to be an exercise in sectarian revenge. By 2007 the U.S. position had become critical: more than 3,000 Americans had died in Iraq, polls showed 72% of the U.S. public no longer supported Bush's handling of the war, the White House was increasing the number of troops on the ground to 150,000, Democrats who had ridden a wave of antiwar sentiment to power in both houses of Congress in November 2006 were attempting to force the White House to begin withdrawing U.S. troops through legislative action—and no end to the conflict was in sight.

On the Gulf, a Natural Disaster Breeds a National Disgrace • 2005

On the morning of Aug. 29, 2005, Hurricane Katrina barreled into the Gulf Coast with wind speeds reaching 127 m.p.h. The storm made landfall near New Orleans, the gracious, historic Louisiana city that lies largely below sea level, protected by a series of aging levees. When those barriers broke, some 80% of the Crescent City was flooded, left; to the east, Mississippi and Alabama cities on the Gulf were also devastated.

Yet the real catastrophe came over the next two weeks: while residents, largely black and largely poor, huddled on their rooftops or at the Superdome athletic complex awaiting rescue, government at all levels seemed to break down. Above, a helicopter rescues a stranded citizen. It took five days for the Federal Emergency Management Administration to evacuate the 25,000 people trapped at the Superdome. More than 1,800 people died in the worst natural disaster in the U.S. since the San Francisco earthquake of 1906, while Katrina drove as many as 1.5 million people from their homes.

SMILEY N. POOL—DALLAS MORNING NEWS—CORBIS; ABOVE: DAVID J. PHILLIP—AP IMAGES

MICHAEL GRECCO

RICH KOSTERS—FOX

DAVID MCNEW—GETTY IMAGES

Click by Click, the Web Changes Everyday Life

Constantly evolving and improving, computer Internet technology continues to reshape society with the speed of a mouse click. In the first years of the 21st century, the World Wide Web began to challenge the power of mainstream media, as "blogs" (short for weblogs) and websites like MySpace and Wikipedia gave everyone with a computer the chance to publish his or her diary, opinions or videos online.

The new empowerment of the audience was reflected on TV, where reality shows like *American Idol,* left, let viewers' votes control the show's outcome via cell-phone voting. The overnight success of the user-driven site YouTube, which allowed individuals to post videos online for free, turned founders Chad Hurley and Steve Chen, above, into instant millionaires—and led TIME to select "You" as its Person of the Year 2006.

Once Again, a Nation Confronts Its Identity

Americans have never stopped arguing over immigration. The nation was largely built by people who came from someplace else, but since the 1790s, each wave of recent arrivals has been trying to lock the door behind them. An estimated 12 million illegal immigrants, the vast majority from Mexico, were living in the U.S. in 2007, and tens of thousands more were arriving each month. Most were clearly violating the law, yet one lesson of U.S. history is that the constant influx of immigrants has been a major engine of the nation's growth. And some sectors of the U.S. economy, such as agriculture, depended on large pools of low-cost labor.

Such clear dichotomies breed controversy: in recent years, many Americans have argued for "zero tolerance" of illegal immigrants, for more immigration officers and for more fences along the U.S.-Mexico border. Others proposed guest-worker programs and the creation of a system to allow longtime illegals to become full citizens. Below, a U.S. border guard eyes illegals who failed to breach the border and are retreating upstream across the New River in Calexico, Calif., in 2006. As of mid-2007, Congress and the Bush Administration were debating a massive overhaul of U.S. immigration policy: 400 years after English settlers at Jamestown looked Powhatan Indians in the eye and pondered the future, their descendants were still asking, "Who gets to be an American?"

Global Warming: A Man-Made Crisis

"It is too soon to tell whether unusual global warming has indeed begun," TIME wrote in 1987. But if the climate did begin to change, the magazine predicted, signs would include "dramatically altered weather patterns, major shifts of deserts and fertile regions, intensification of tropical storms and a rise in sea level." Two decades later, it is no longer too soon to tell. The future is now.

Few people listened in the 1890s when Svante Arrhenus, a little-known Swedish chemist, issued a warning: if humans kept pumping carbon dioxide (CO_2) into the air, as they had begun doing at the dawn of the industrial age, around 1750, the increase in heat-trapping gas in the atmosphere would raise temperatures dramatically.

More than 100 years later, the validity of Arrhenus' thesis is borne out in the headlines every day. Droughts and wildfires, floods and crop failures, receding glaciers and images of drowning polar bears, the destruction of New Orleans by Hurricane Katrina and the growing list of reports by alarmed scientists: the trickle of events and evidence has become a torrent, firmly demonstrating that global warming is a serious, worldwide crisis.

The heat is only continuing to rise. The year 2006 was the hottest on record in the U.S. Of the 12 warmest years on record, 11 occurred between 1995 and 2006. Those numbers reflect a more ominous trend: atmospheric levels of CO_2 were 379 parts per million in 2005, higher than at any time in the past 650,000 years. At right, tourists at the visitors center at Alaska's Portage Valley can no longer see the Portage Glacier, which has receded drastically since the center was built in 1986; instead, they see icebergs floating in the bay.

If the diagnosis is in, what's the cure? The antidote for global warming, if there is one, will inevitably include two indispensable ingredients: a willingness to face unpleasant facts, and the political will to take whatever actions are necessary to address them.

262

Index

264

Fort Sumter, 64, 65
Foster, Stephen, 50
France
    colonies, 8
    Louisiana Purchase and, 26, 27
    Statue of Liberty, 116
    Vichy France, 179
    World War I, 149, 151, 152
    World War II, 177, 179, 180
Franco, Francisco, 179
Frankensteen, Richard, 173
Franklin, Benjamin, 9, 12, 17, 20–21, 122
Franklin stove, 21
Fredericksburg, Battle of, 68
Freedom Riders, 214, 215
Frémont, John C., 47
French and Indian War, 8
Frick, Henry Clay, 140
Fuchs, Klaus, 191
Fugitive Slave Act, 58, 59
Fulton, Robert, 36

G

Gangbusters (radio show), 174
Gangsta rap, 251
Gardner, Alexander, 76
Garibaldi Guard, 71
Gates, Bill, 241
George Washington, 13
Georgia, 63
Germany
    Hindenburg, 175
    immigration from, 35
    World War I, 149, 151
    World War II, 177, 180
Geronimo, 83, 99
Gershwin, George, 157
Gettysburg, Battle of, 77
Gettysburg Address, 77
Ghost Dance, 98
Gilded Age, 112–15
Gillette, King, 146
Ginsberg, Allen, 203
Giuliani, Rudolph, 253
Glenn, John, 220
Goldman, Ronald, 249
Gold Rush
    California, 46–47
    Montana, 89
    Yukon, 101
Gone With the Wind (film), 175
Gorbachev, Mikhail, 237
Gore, Al, 255
Gould, Jay, 114, 115
Goyathlay (Geronimo), 99
Grabill, John C.H., 93
Graham, Billy, 201
Grange, Red, 165
Grant, Ulysses S., 66, 72, 73, 77, 79
Grapes of Wrath, The (Steinbeck), 170
Grateful Dead, 205
Grattan Massacre, 95
Great Depression, 140, 166–76
Great Plains, 90
Great Society, 210
Great War. *See* World War I
Great White Fleet, 134–35
Gretzky, Wayne, 243
Griffith, D.W., 162, 163
Guadalcanal, 182
Guam, 129, 133, 182
Guantánamo Bay, 129
Gulf War, 247
Guthrie, Woody, 170

H

Halas, George, 165
Hall, Jerry, 230
Hamilton, Alexander, 18, 19

Hamlin, Hannibal, 61
Hampton Roads, Battle of, 68
Hanna, Mark, 136
Harburg, E.Y., 167
Harlem Renaissance, 161
Harper's Weekly, 100
Harrison, William Henry, 30, 83
Harry, Debbie, 230
Hawaii, 132, 133
    Pearl Harbor, 177, 182
Hawthorne, Nathaniel, 50, 51
Hayes, Rutherford B., 123
Haymarket Riot, 123
Helena, Mont., 88–89
Hessians, 14
Hickok, James (Wild Bill), 91
Hinckley, John, Jr., 237
Hindenburg, 175
Hine, Lewis W., ii, 141
hippies, 216, 219, 230
Hiroshima, 186
Hitler, Adolf, 177, 179, 180
Ho Chi Minh, 210
Holland, 177
Hollywood
    Red Scare and, 190
    film industry established, 162
homesteaders, 100
Hoover, Herbert, 168
Hoover, J. Edgar, 174
Hoovervilles, 168
Houdini, Harry, 160
Houston, Sam, 42, 43
Howl (Ginsberg), 203
Howland, M., 67
Hubble, Edwin, 239
Hubble Space Telescope, 239
Hudson River, 36
Hurricane Katrina, 258–59

I

"I Have a Dream" speech (King), 215, 218
I Love Lucy, 202
IBM, 199, 241
Idaho, 41, 44
immigrants and immigration, 116, 134
    backlash against, 35
    Civil War soldiers, 71
    quotas, 138
imperialism in U.S., 126–33
incandescent lightbulb, 110
indentured servants, 6
Indian Territory, 100
Industrial Workers of the World, 140
influenza epidemic, 154–55
International Business Machines (IBM), 199
Internet, 249
interstate highway system, 193
Intrepid (balloon), 70
Iran, Shah of, 232
Iran-*contra* scheme, 236, 237
Iran hostage crisis, 222, 232, 236
Iraq war, 256–57
Irish Americans
    Civil War and, 71
    discrimination against, 35, 116
ironclad ships, 68
iron curtain, 186
Iroquois Confederacy, 8
Irving, Washington, 39
isolationism, 150, 177
Israel, 232, 245, 247
Ives, James M., 119
Iwo Jima, 182, 183

J

Jackson, Andrew, 28, 34

Jackson, "Drummer," 67
Jackson, Michael, 242
Jackson, Thomas (Stonewall), 65, 73
James, Jesse, 91
Jamestown, Va., 6, 7
Japan
    Gulf War and, 245, 247
    World War II, 177, 186
    Japanese Americans, World War II internment of, 184
Jaws (film), 231
Jay, John, 17, 19
jazz age, 160
jazz music, 161, 194
Jazz Singer, The (film) 163
Jefferson, Isaac, 23
Jefferson, Thomas, 5, 12, 18, 21, 23, 24, 25, 26, 27, 44, 53
Jemison, Edwin E., 67
Jim Crow laws, 123, 214
jingoism, 126, 129, 133, 137
Jobs, Steven, 241
Johnson, Lyndon B., 210, 218
Johnson, Magic, 243
Johnstown Flood, 121
Jolson, Al, 163
Jones, Bobby, 165
Jones, Cleve, 240
Joplin, Janis, 217
Jordan, Michael, 243
Joseph, Chief, 82
Jungle, The (Sinclair), 138

K

Kamehameha I, 132
Kansas, 171
Kansas-Nebraska Act, 58
Kaposi's sarcoma, 240
Karzai, Hamid, 255
Kelso, William, 6
Kennedy, Jacqueline, 206, 209, 210
Kennedy, John F., 206–10, 214, 220
Kennedy, Robert, 218
Kentucky, 22, 63
Kerouac, Jack, 203
Key, Francis Scott, 29
Keystone Kops, 157
Khomeini, Ayatullah Ruhollah, 232, 236
Khrushchev, Nikita, 191, 207
Kindred Spirits (Durand), 39
kinetescope, 111
King, Martin Luther, Jr., 139, 200, 218
Know-Nothing Party, 35
Kodak cameras, 109, 146
Korean War, 189
Ku Klux Klan, 159, 163
Kuwait, 245, 247

L

labor issues
    child labor, 141
    immigrants, 138
    Supreme Court and, 112
    unions, 123, 140
    violence, 123, 173
Lafayette, Marquis de, 16
Lakota, 83, 93
Lange, Dorothea, 170
Lardner, Ring, Jr., 190
Laughlin, T.P., 152
League of Nations, 150
Leaves of Grass (Whitman), 50
Lee, Robert E., 66, 72, 73, 74, 77, 79, 80
Lee, Spike, 59
Lend Lease policy, 177
L'Enfant, Pierre, 18
LeRoy, Mervyn, 163
Leutze, Emanuel, 15

Lewinsky, Monica, 249
Lewis, Carl, 243
Lewis, Meriwether, 26, 27
Lewis and Clark expedition, 27
Lichtenstein, Roy, 217
light bulb, 110
lightning rod, 21
Liliuokalani, Queen, 132
Lincoln, Abraham, 53, 61, 62, 64, 68, 70, 73, 74, 77, 79, 80, 123, 236
Lindbergh, Charles, 157, 164
Little Big Horn, Battle of, 83, 94–95, 95
Little Rock Central High School, 200, 214
Longfellow, Mary, 86
Los Angeles, 219
Louis, Joe, 185
Louisiana, 63
Louisiana Purchase, 26, 27, 31, 44
Louisiana Territory, 25
Lowell Offering, The, 48
LSD, 205
Lucas, George, 231
Luce, Henry, 134
Lumière brothers, 111

M

MacArthur, Douglas, 189
Madison, James, 10, 18, 19, 28
Madonna, 235, 242
Maine, 31
Malvern Hill, Battle of, 67
Manifest Destiny, 40, 45, 96
Manson, Charles, 219
March on Washington (1963), 215, 218
marijuana, 216
Marshall Plan, 186
Marx Brothers, 157
"Masters of the Universe," 235
Material Girl, 235
Mauchly, J.W., 199
Mauldin, Bill, 180
McAuliffe, Christa, 238
McCarthy, Joseph, 190
McCarty, Henry (Billy the Kid), 91
McClellan, George B., 61, 68, 73, 74
McKinley, William, 133, 136, 210
McLernand, John A., 63
McVeigh, Timothy, 249
"Me decade," 29, 235
Medicare, 210
Melville, Herman, 50, 51
Menjou, Adolf, 190
Mercury astronaut program, 220
Meuse-Argonne Offensive, 152
Mexico
    Mexican Cession, 45
    Mexican War, 41, 42–43, 44, 45, 47
Microsoft, 241
Midway, Battle of, 182
Miniconjou Sioux, 98
minstrel shows, 59
Mississippi, 63
Missouri, 63
Missouri Compromise, 31, 59
Moby Dick (Melville), 50
Model T Ford, 147
Monopoly (game), 175
Montana, 172
Montcalm, Marquis, 8
Montgomery bus boycott, 200, 214, 218
Monticello, 23
moon landing, 220
Moore, Clement C., 39
Moore, Scotty, 196

Morgan, J.P., 114
Morse, Samuel, 109
Morse Code, 109
Morse telegraph, 109
Mott, Lucretia, 48, 139
Mount Suribachi, 183
MTV, 242
muckrakers, 138
Murrah, Alfred P., Federal Building, 249
Murrow, Edward R., 190
Mussolini, Benito, 179
My Lai massacre, 211

N

Nagasaki, 186
Napoléon Bonaparte, 27
Nast, Thomas, 115
Natchez & Hamburg Railroad, 36–37
National Aeronautics and Space Administration (NASA), 221, 238, 239
National Broadcasting Corp., 160
National Football League, 165
National Organization for Women (NOW), 228
National Recovery Administration (NRA), 172
Native Americans. *See also* specific peoples
    ancestors, 5
    early encounters with Europeans, 5
    French and Indian War, 8
    Indian Territory, 100
    Little Big Horn, 83, 94–95
    "removal" of, 35, 82, 83
    smallpox and, 93
    Trail of Tears, 35
    Wounded Knee massacre, 98
"nativist" movement, 35
Navajo, 83, 93
Negro League (baseball), 185
Nelson, Gaylord, 227
Neutrality Act, 177
Nevada, 44
New Deal, 168, 172–73, 210
New Frontier, 206
New Mexico, 171
New Mexico Territory, 58
New Orleans, 161, 259
New Orleans, Battle of, 28
Newport Folk Festival, 217
New World
    European attitudes toward, 3
    European exploration of, 5
New York City
    immigration, 116
    political corruption, 115
New York Times, 229
Nicaragua, 237
Nixon, Richard, 206, 222, 223, 229
North, Oliver, 237
North Atlantic Treaty Organization (NATO), 186
North Carolina, 63
North Korea, 189
North Pacific Railroad, 96
North Vietnam, 210–13, 222, 225
Northwest Indian War, 22
Northwest Territory, 22
Norway, 177
Notes on the State of Virginia (Jefferson), 23
nuclear bomb, 191
nuclear power, 186

O

Oakley, Annie, 103
Oh! Calcutta!, 229

265

Index

266

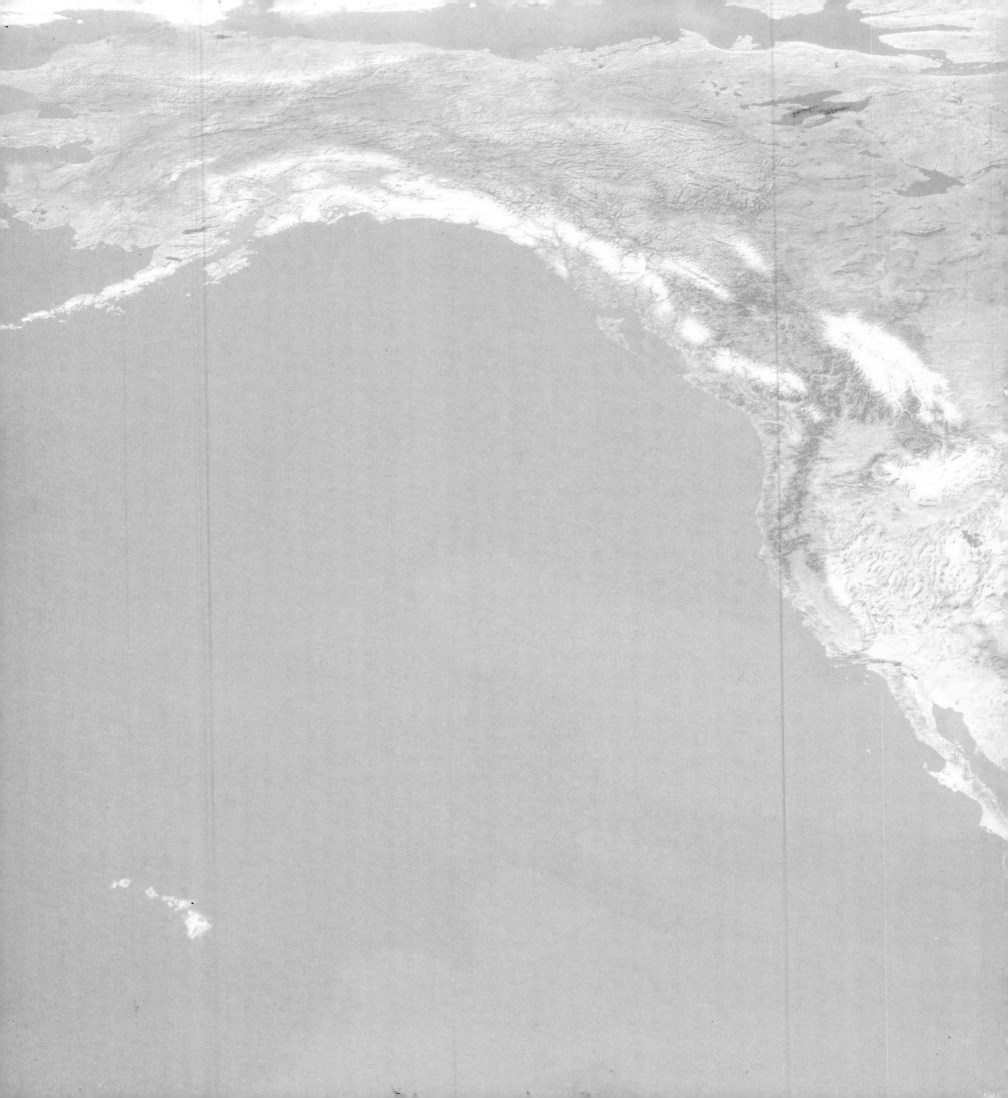